Often when I read books, I'm not quite sure what the author's main point is, so I find myself racking my brain to figure out what they are trying to communicate at both the book level and chapter level. This can be frustrating and time-consuming, so when I write, I want the main idea of what I am trying to communicate to be as clear as possible.

To make it easier for my readers, I include a section that explicitly summarizes the book into one simple concept. For example, in my first book, *2 Second Lean*, the goal was to teach the reader to "learn to see waste." In my second book, *Lean Health*, I wanted you to "treat your body like you would treat a Ferrari." With *Lean Travel*, I want to show you how to "travel light with a full heart." *(Go to the link at the end of this section to find out more about 2 Second Lean and Lean Health.)*

In addition to summarizing the entire book with one phrase, I put a simple, to-the-point summary at the end of every chapter called "The One Thing." It is a phrase that captures the essence of the chapter. Feel free to skip ahead and read "The One Thing" first before you even read the chapter—whatever works best for you. The important thing is that you can easily and quickly understand what it is I'm trying to say.

-Enjoy the read!

What's the one thing? Paul

Complexity sucks!

The One Thing:
Keep everything in life as simple as possible.

paulakers.net/lt-one

Preface

Travel Light with a Full Heart

Sitting in the breakfast area at a resort in Phuket, Thailand, I noticed that all the other guests were eating, talking with friends, or working on their phones, and paying little attention to the amazing people taking care of them. Absorbed in their own lives, they didn't bother to acknowledge the people keeping their food fresh, picking up their plates, offering to refill their glasses, and cleaning up after them when they left. As they finished, most walked away without even a glance to say thank you.

For some reason, I found it easy to put myself in the workers' shoes that day. I was humbled by the thought that most of them had woken very early in the morning to make sure everything was ready for us. How nice it would be for someone just to smile at them and say thank you!

Phuket, Thailand

Over the years, I've concluded that there are two kinds of people in the world: givers and takers. Takers are always looking to extract whatever they can from life and are less interested in what they can contribute. They are self-absorbed, they only care about themselves. Givers, on the other hand, are actively thinking about other people. Givers live by the idea that you "first give and then you may receive."

In my opinion, it is much better to be a giver than a taker. About ten years ago, I decided that I wanted to become a world-class giver who. Surrounded myself with other world-class givers, and to get all the takers the hell out of my life as quickly as possible. Since then, I've successfully done this and the quality of my life has improved dramatically. Now, everywhere I go people ask me, "Paul why are you doing what you're doing? You spend so much time helping other people learn about Lean and improve their organizations and you ask for so little in return!"

I always work hard to get to know people on my travels. These two beautiful ladies did a fantastic job preparing my fish and making my smoothies everyday during my stay in Phuket, Thailand.

The answer is simple: I understand the power of being a giver, and in order to have a rich life you must first learn to give.

At this point, you might be thinking, "Why are you telling me this at the beginning of a book called *Lean Travel*?" The reason is quite simple, in order to have a great travel experience, you must approach it from the standpoint that you are going to treat all the people you encounter with dignity and respect, understanding that they are working hard to help you have a great trip. If you regularly give them your respect, your smile, your encouragement, and your gratitude, your travel will be a blessing!

In addition to being grateful, another way to make your travel experience more fulfilling is to live by the adage that "less is more." In a Lean Travel context, this means to travel light. For example, I once bought a pair of high-quality Keen sandals, thinking they would be the ultimate travel sandal. After a few trips around the world, however, I realized they were really quite bulky and heavy. They were also a little bit of an overkill for when I needed sandals, which was mostly just when walking to my hotel's pool or to the restaurant for breakfast.

So, in adherence to my philosophy of traveling light, I found a very inexpensive pair of sandals for $5 and I turned in my $70 pair of Keens. This is a perfect example of Lean Travel because it demonstrates how a simple two-second improvement can make travel more effective and enjoyable. My suitcase weighed about four pounds less, everything packed up easier, and the new sandals were absolutely perfect for my needs.

Less is more. A small improvement that made traveling light and easy

As you start this book, I want you to understand the two main parts of my *Lean Travel* philosophy. First, what you give and the fullness of your heart toward the people you encounter on your travel experience will have a profound impact on how much you enjoy it. Second, the less you bring and the lighter you travel, the more you will be able to feel and adapt to the fantastic trade winds of the travel experience. So, travel light with a full heart!

> **The One Thing:**
> Be a world-class giver, surround yourself with givers and get all takers the hell out of your life as fast as you can.

paulakers.net/lt-preface

Paul A. Akers

FastCap Press

Copyright © 2016 by FastCap Press
All rights reserved,
including the right of reproduction
in whole or in part in any form.

For information about special discounts for bulk purchases, please contact
Paul Akers: 888-443-3748 or paul@paulakers.net

Written by Paul Akers
First printing, July 2016
Manufactured in the United States of America

Lean Travel comes in ALL flavors

You can read it or get even more insight by watching the videos and reviewing the resources on PaulAkers.net. Or listen to the expanded Audio-Book with extra "off-script" inspiration and added stories of innovation.

Check out PaulAkers.net for all the latest Lean Adventures

paulakers.net/lt

Acknowledgments

Editors

Leanne Akers and Lori Turley who edited the original manuscript.

Graphics & Book Layout

Jayme Newby

Special Thanks

    In my second book, *Lean Health*, I mentioned how my great friend and Brazilian beauty, Paloma, challenged me to make no excuses and to start writing *Lean Health* immediately. Now, only a few months after publishing *Lean Health*, Sara Bailey (wife of the witty Brit, Ashley Bailey) assumed the role Paloma had taken and said in a Facebook post, "Paul, you need to write *Lean Travel*." Without giving me even a few seconds to digest this crazy thought, the ever-annoying Ashley also typed, "No excuses buddy! You need to get *Lean Travel* written and published by my birthday, May 17!"

    I asked him if he was kidding, because I was way too busy to add that to my plate, since May 17 was only six months away. However, it seems that every time I say I am too busy, or that something can't be done, I am confronted with my own words that I give other people, "Stop making excuses!"

    Ashley is not a girl, so he definitely lacks some of the persuasive powers that Paloma and Sara have, but he is a competent businessman and fellow Lean maniac, as well as a close friend who can be a real pain in my butt, particularly when he threatens me with consequences if I don't get something done by his birthday. (The details of the threat will go unsaid for the time being, but perhaps they will be revealed someday in one of my future musings.)

Sara & Ashley Bailey with Katie and William Bailey

    So, Ashley and Sara, this book would never have happened without you. Sara, thank you for the nudge, and Ashley, for kicking my ass!

Contents

Authors Note:	The One Thing	1
Preface:	Travel Light with a Full Heart	2
Intro:	A Quick Look at Lean Thinking	9
Chapter 1:	Lean Travel is Remarkable Travel	15
Chapter 2:	My Warped Perspective on Travel	20
Chapter 3:	Less is More	27
Chapter 4:	Debacle in Dubai	33
Chapter 5:	Just-In-Time Travel	40
Chapter 6:	Always	52
Chapter 7:	The Experienced Traveler	68
Chapter 8:	All we need is Fat Navy SEALs	74
Chapter 9:	Horse's Ass or Diplomat	81
Chapter 10:	Know the Facts, Understand the Details	96
Chapter 11:	Details	104
Chapter 12:	It's A Very Small World	122

paulakers.net/lt-resources

What's This?

In the Digital copy of Lean Travel, this orange bar will link you to the videos and resources Paul has created on all his Travels. The inspiring videos will get you all excited to explore the world with everything you will learn in *Lean Travel*.

paulakers.net

Step 1
Click or Type the web-link into your browser.

Step 2
Select the Books tab, then select *Lean Travel*, then select Resources by Chapter

Step 3
Select the Chapter you would like to view

Step 4
After selecting the Chapter, you will see a list of resources, plus the videos that are associated with the chapter

Step 5
Under the books tab you can find all available electronic versions of Lean Travel **FOR FREE!**

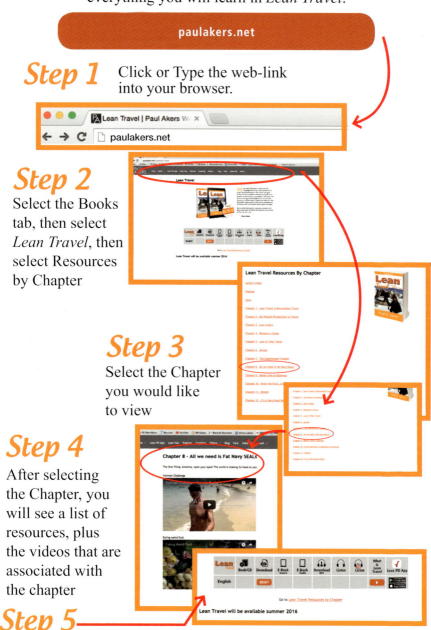

A Quick Look at Lean Thinking

Intro

In my first book, *2 Second Lean*, I wrote about how I learned to build a fun, continuously improving Lean culture in my company, FastCap. To make Lean more accessible to everyone, I simplified the Lean principles of continuous improvement. After successfully implementing Lean at FastCap, I shared what we had learned with others. Thousands of

FastCap

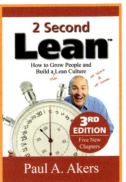

2 Second Lean

companies and managers worldwide wanted to learn a simplified way of implementing Lean. The simple ideas that I laid out in *2 Second Lean* helped them run and manage their organizations at a much higher level. In these companies, tens of thousands of employees are more engaged as they go about their work each day. They do a better job of serving their customers and constantly improving their products, all while reducing costs, increasing profits and wages, and creating greater job security in a team environment where everyone wins.

Taking the same Lean principles and applying them to my health was the inspiration for my second book. *Lean Health* tells the story of how I achieved exceptional health by treating my body like a Ferrari. I was an average, overweight 54-year-old man who transformed himself into a high-performance machine. After the transformation I looked like I could be on the cover of Men's Health magazine. By applying daily small improvements over a one-year period, I refined and simplified the process of managing my health, eliminated the waste in my diet and exercise regimen, and turned my life clock back twenty years.

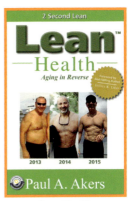

Lean Health

My third book, *Lean Travel*, is about how I tamed the struggle of travel. In this book I will show you how I applied Lean principles in a new way, in order to improve every aspect of the travel experience. *(Go to the link at the end of this chapter to find out more about 2 Second Lean, Lean Health and FastCap.)*

One of the main goals of Lean is to identify and eliminate waste. Most people tolerate a great deal of waste when they travel. They wait in lines at the ticket counter and at security, which forces them to arrive much earlier than their departure time. They wait to pick up their luggage, which does not always arrive when and where it is supposed to. They continue to wait more at the rental counter as attendants slowly work through lines of customers, clicking through the options on their screens and trying to upsell drivers on high-fee (and unnecessary) extra purchases.

Such a waste waiting in long lines

As a Lean thinker, I view theses wastes as a beautiful opportunity to improve my life. I want perfection when I travel, and though I know it will never be perfect, I will get much closer than most people think is possible. I want my travel experience to be focused on learning and meeting people and not be distracted by the clunky mechanics of getting somewhere.

I do this because I am passionate about travel. I have been to 60 countries and have the goal of traveling to 100 countries by the age of 65. I am an instrument-rated pilot and have flown my own plane across the North Atlantic multiple times. I've landed at hundreds of airports all over the world, and have seen sides of travel that most people don't even know exist—from private FBOs (fixed based operators) catering to corporate aircraft of the rich and famous, to landing on dirt runways in Africa. (Before you dismiss me as some rich guy who can afford things most cannot, I recently sold my airplane and now travel only commercially, and 90% is in economy class. I book all my own travel arrangements and don't have a travel agent or assistant managing my crazy travel schedule.) I travel about six months of the year and commonly take trips that last between two weeks and two months.

This book charts my journey of continually improving the way I travel. It describes how I think about leaning out the process of travel and continue to improve it every day, every leg, every hotel check-in and every trip I make. I have worked hard to simplify every aspect of travel and remove the mountains of waste so my travel experience can be pure joy.

In order to Lean out your travels and simplify everything you do, you must have a deep understanding of the eight wastes:

1. Overproduction
2. Transportation
3. Inventory
4. Defects
5. Over-processing
6. Motion
7. Waiting
8. Wasted human potential

Here's a quick example of how the eight wastes manifest themselves in the travel experience, using a very common travel item: soap.

Overproduction

When we check into a hotel, our rooms have a little bar of soap at the sink and another one for the shower. During our stay, between washing our hands and bathing ourselves, we might use 10% of the soap the hotel has provided. As a result, the hotel has to purchase much more soap than is actually necessary for its customers.

Those damn little bars of soap

Transportation

Billions of mini soap bars are used all over the world each year, which means that a lot of unnecessary transportation is needed to move it all. The waste of transporting the soap to the hotel, and then to the garbage can, the dumpster, and then to landfills really adds up! Added to this is the transportation waste of the D9 Caterpillar that runs back and forth, burying mountains of overproduced soap at the landfill, as well as the transportation of the fuel and the maintenance vehicles that service the D9 Caterpillars.

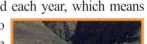

Damn little bars of soap put into landfills

Inventory

In addition to the excess soap inventory being held and managed in landfills around the world, hotels must deal with an abundance of soap in supply rooms. Managing the excess soap inventory is a waste.

Unnecessary inventory of those damn little bars of soap

Defects

The soap leaves scum on the sink and on the tray in the shower. The resulting mess is a defect that requires the housekeeping staff to do extra work.

Over-processing

Waste begets more waste and now we're adding things to the travel process that have nothing to do with why the product process was originally put in place. The purpose of providing soap is so guests can clean and sanitize their hands and avoid spreading germs, not to create mountains of motion and inventory because someone was not thoughtful about the way they set up the procedure in the first place.

Motion

The entire process of managing these little bars of soap produces mountains of wasted motion. From getting the bars of soap from the supply room onto the cleaning cart, to moving the cart into the room, to retrieving the unused bars and throwing them into the trash can and then emptying the trash can. The list goes on and on.

Those damn little bars of soap cause mountains of wasted motion

Waiting

I can't tell you the number of times I have checked into a hotel early around 10:00 a.m. and have been told my room will not be ready until one or two o'clock in the afternoon. Why? Because management has made the housekeeping staff perform silly procedures that have no value for the customer (e.g., moving tiny bars of soaps around), and because management can't see the wastes in what they are asking their team to perform every day.

Wasted human potential

This is the greatest waste of all—when you have a human being that's capable of so much and you make them do mundane, repetitive, stupid work (like managing excess soap) instead of teaching them to use their brain to continuously improve. The hotel staff members are dealing with soap when they could be doing more important work. This is the worst tragedy and the biggest of all the eight wastes and it's happening all over the world every day.*(Go to the link at the end of this chapter to find a diagram of the 8 wastes.)*

So what? You say. It's just soap! Who cares?

You should care, because you're paying for that waste, whether you like it or not. Nobody works for free. Hotels just pass the cost of their stupidity on to you. (If, by chance, you're someone who thinks that part of the privilege of traveling is to open up a new bar of soap every day, then there's nothing I can do for you. But let me say this: Waste is not elegant or glamorous! Waste is ignorance.)

In addition to showing you how I travel, this book will give you the tools and understanding to make Lean Travel something that is fun and easy for you. No matter what your lot in life is, being born into this generation during this time period is the greatest gift that any human being could ever have. Opportunities are endless, and the world is open for business. Countries like Burma, China, Cambodia, Cuba, Kazakhstan and Sri Lanka (places Westerners used to avoid) are today wide open and, for the most part, welcoming. They have fantastic historical sites and the full spectrum of accommodations, from cheap hostels to five-star resorts. Come along, we have a world to discover and amazing friends to make along the way!

By the way, much of the waste involved with the mini soap bars could be solved with either of two easy solutions:

First, hotels could put liquid soap dispensers on the sink and in the shower. The customer would use only what they need. The dispensers could be designed to clearly indicate when they are running low so that the housekeeping staff could refill them only when necessary. Already, I'm seeing this more and more in hotels around the world, particularly in Asia, where people realize that resources are finite and they had better figure out a way to use them more efficiently.

Another great example of strong visual controls in the elimination of those damn little bars of soap.

Bring your own soap. It is faster, easier, and a lot less waste!

Second, travelers can solve the problem themselves. I have a small soap container that I put one of those little mini bars of soap in. When I check into the hotel, I simply open my shaving kit and I have my personal mini bar of soap that lasts me for a couple weeks. That's a 1,400 percent improvement over the current system!

Lean solutions that companies all over the world are starting to do. Simple and effective! Wall mounted soap dispensers in by the sink and in shower.

Notice the position of the on/off valve on the shower. Somebody used their brain and improved an age old standard that made it difficult for billions of people around the world to turn on the water in the shower. Finally, we don't have to bend over and get wet. The power of thinking Lean. Could you imagine what the world would look like if everybody did this?

Noticed this clever improvement. Instead of reaching into the shower to turn the water on, they cut a hole in the side of the glass so you never get wet until you're ready to. All improvements like this make life so much easier and at the same time put a smile on your face.

The One Thing:
Being wasteful is not glamorous. It is the epitome of ignorance.

paulakers.net/lt-intro

Chapter 1

Lean Travel is remarkable travel!

Lean travel is remarkable travel. Why? It is easy, rewarding, and (almost always) stress-free. *Lean Travel* helps you create the kind of travel experience that when people look at the way you do things, they say, "Wow, that's cool! How do you do that?" I tell them it's not complicated. All you have to do is continuously improve everything you do and apply Lean principles to the way you travel.

Look how easy it is for me to manage charging my electronic devices everytime I walk into a hotel room

As a Lean thinker, I have greatly improved my life with one very simple idea, one that even a four year-old could understand: Everything in life is a process. Think about it—making your bed, brushing your teeth, managing your e-mails, paying your bills, shopping for groceries, washing your clothes, cutting the grass, traveling—all are processes. Each one of these activities has a starting point and a completion point, with several steps in between. When doing any of them, you encounter waste that doesn't add value to what you're trying to accomplish. *(Go to the link at the end of this chapter to see how Paul organizes his electrical cords.)*

One thing to plug in and all electronic devices are ready to be charged

Quick, easy, and simple to set up and to take down. Nothing to manage except a great process.

For example, let's say it's laundry day at your house and it is your turn to wash the clothes. As you start a load, you reach down in a cabinet to pick up the detergent bottle, screw off the cap, set it on the edge of the machine, pour a little in, replace the cap (dribbling a little on the machine in the process), put the bottle back in the cabinet, and close the door. You reach up, adjust the load settings, and finally, start the machine. You're not done yet, though. You still must wipe up the spilled soap with

Spot the waste, remove the waste, and improve your life

a towel and toss it into the laundry to be washed with the next load.

Of all those steps, the only value-added one is putting the soap into the machine, which should take a total of three seconds. Everything else is non-value-added activity—waste! There is plenty of wasted motion (bending down and up and down), unnecessary transportation (of the soap to and from the cabinet), over-processing (taking off the cap and replacing it), and a defect (the spill) that robs you of ten seconds of your precious time on this earth—without getting your clothes any cleaner!

Paul great improvement! My 92 year old mom loves Lean

What could you do to simplify this process? At my 92 year old mother's house, my solution was to put the laundry soap on a shelf right above the washing machine. The bottle has a little button you push to let the soap come out and a cap that doubles as a small measuring cup. Previously, my mom used this cup for every laundry load. She would pour soap into it, walk over to the machine and dump the soap in, then go back and place the cup next to the detergent. With the soap now above the washer, my mother could remove the cup from the process by opening the washer door, pushing the button, and counting to three. Voila! A process that took her twenty seconds now takes her three, and she doesn't have to worry about spilling or dropping the measuring cup. When people see how my mom washes her clothes, they comment on how it's really smart. Indeed, Lean is really smart and makes it surprisingly easy to improve processes, if you apply a little common sense and a few basic principles.

So much that you do in life is a process, and even seemingly insignificant processes contain some degree of waste. For example, I'm writing this book on my Mac, and as I finish each chapter, I let the Text-To-Speech feature read it back to me so I can hear the cadence of my words. The usual process for making this happen has four steps: highlight the text, right click, select Speak, then select Speak Text.

Text-To-Speech on Mac

Step 1: Go to System Preferences and select Dictation & Speech

Step 2: Check Speak Selected Text when the key is pressed

Step 3: Press Option+S, and your Mac will speak to you!

With my big hands, it can sometimes be a little bit of a struggle to do this without making a mistake and having to repeat the entire process. Each time I mess up, I am wasting a few seconds of my valuable time, and even more important, I get a tiny bit agitated. (For the love of God, don't get Paul agitated!)

After bungling the steps about thirty times, I finally decided to improve the process. I went into Settings and created a shortcut so that all I have to do to enable the text-to-speech function is to hit Command+S. It is so simple and it works perfectly every time. I took a process that was four seconds (with a high probability of making an error) and shortened it to one second (and made it nearly error-free). That is at least a 400% improvement! Thanks to one small change, writing this book will go more smoothly, there will be fewer defects in the final editing process, and I get the satisfaction of making yet another improvement in my life. When you can stack small improvements up like this day after day, you begin to see why I am a Lean fanatic. They help my life get better every single day. *(Go to the link at the end of this chapter to find out how to set up Text-to-speech on your computer.)*

You can do the same thing with travel. When you go somewhere, you deal with so many processes that could be improved. Imagine preparing for a trip, either in your own country or perhaps somewhere far away. So much goes into getting ready: dreaming about the trip, researching, planning, booking flights, finding a hotel, figuring out where to go and how much time to spend at each place, updating passports and visas, deciding which clothes to take, planning and communicating with the people you will meet on the other side of the world, getting to the airport, going through security, enduring flight delays, navigating unfamiliar airports and transportation systems, finding restaurants, tipping—the list goes on and on! With so many different variables there are many opportunities for things to get fouled up, but there are at least as many opportunities to create your own small improvements.

This is why I am excited about *Lean Travel*—it leads to remarkable experiences by removing the waste from the processes affecting your travel. As you learn how to do it, you will have more time to get that perfect picture, to sip that fantastic cappuccino in the cozy coffee shop in Portugal, to take that beautiful walk on the beach by your hotel in Costa Rica, or to learn salsa at that dance studio hidden among the cobblestone streets of Havana. Lean Travel leads to less misunderstanding, fewer missed flights, and more thank-god-I-have-some-extra-time-to-go-see-these-amazing-historical-sites moments. Applying Lean thinking to travel (to anything, really) makes so much sense and makes everything so much better.

Lean Travel will lead to having the most remarkable experience of all time

So the goal: to consider every step you take while traveling as a process to be improved. The results will put a smile on your face that changes your travel experience and your life forever!

The One Thing:
Everything in life is a process. Make small daily improvements and your life will be remarkable.

paulakers.net/lt-01

Chapter 2

My Warped perspective on travel

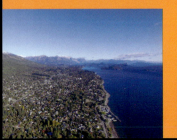

Around 2005, I began to travel quite extensively for my company. Every time I turned around, I found myself walking into an airport, waiting for a plane to take off, or dealing with flight delays. I'm an impatient person to begin with, but having to deal with the flight schedules and all the issues surrounding travel frustrated me to no end.

To further complicate things, I live in Bellingham, Washington, a small town, whose airport has only a few outbound flights each day. All of my trips had to go through Seattle, which added three to four hours to the length of every trip. If I drove to Seattle, it cost me two hours of road time plus the expense of parking. Then, if I happened to return late at night, I faced another two-hour drive while being drop-dead tired. Flying to Seattle didn't save much time either, because I had to get to the airport an hour early for all my flights.

One day, I stopped at a convenience store in the Seattle airport to look for something to read and picked out a magazine called Flying. On the front cover was this amazing-looking airplane called a JetProp, next to a headline that said, "Business or Pleasure." One of the articles inside compared flying from Seattle to Southern California in a private plane versus flying on a commercial airline. The author said it was just as fast to take your

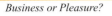
Business or Pleasure?

own plane as it was to fly commercially. I was a bit skeptical about the claim at first, but after reading the whole article, I realized I

Efficient travel is a big deal to me as you can see. I took it very seriously with a major investment of my time and resources...Little did I know there was a much better way.

Paul's magic carpet. **Left**: *Paul's first Diamond DA40.* **Right**: *Paul's second plane JetProp*

could benefit from having my own plane. Since Bellingham is only a half-hour flight from Seattle, I could save myself a few hours on nearly every business trip, and also cut out some of the clunky mechanics of traveling commercially. I spent the rest of the trip (to Southern California, coincidentally) thinking about the possibilities of becoming a pilot.

Paul traveling all over the world visiting customers and clients and making travel just a little bit easier in his busy schedule

After a year of researching the pros and cons of owning a plane, I decided to pull the trigger and get my pilot's license. Soon thereafter, I bought my first plane, a Diamond DA40. A year and a half later, I bought the plane of my dreams: a JetProp similar to the one on the magazine cover. The turbine aircraft could fly at 28,000 feet and almost 300 miles an hour. Soon, I was jetting all over the United States and Europe, logging thousands of hours behind the controls of my new plane. *(Go to the link at the end of this chapter to watch Paul's flight adventures.)*

In those days, flying my own aircraft made a lot of sense. Many of my distributors were in small communities scattered across the United States, and it was convenient to fly directly to nearby regional airports that weren't served by the commercial airlines. Over the next ten years, I spent a lot of time flying myself around, never needing to schedule an airline

Paul, pilot in command, lots of responsibilities

ticket or worry about whether there was a connecting flight to some obscure airport.

The convenience was great, but it came with a high price tag. It was expensive to learn to fly and to maintain two aircraft. Another big expense was bringing a professional pilot along with me much of the time, just to make sure I did everything right. (The kind of flying I was doing was very complex—it was not unusual for me to fly to five states in one day.) My entire foray into private aviation served me well, but about a year ago, I decided to sell my planes. While I certainly enjoyed having them and the experiences they provided me, I now reflect back on that time period and realize I had a warped perspective on travel.

What I thought was a long list of inconveniences . . .

I used to think about commercial travel as nothing but a long list of inconveniences—crowded seats, bad food, flight delays, etc. Today though, I feel entirely different about it. Because I have learned Lean and know how to eliminate waste in everything, travel has become pure joy for me. When I have to go somewhere, I look forward to traveling commercially. In fact, I now see commercial travel as better than private because I don't have to manage an aircraft, an aviation department, or anything else. I can just leave all that to the pros who have a much better safety and track record than I could ever accomplish. (Even though I had no accidents or any problems, the training of a professional pilot far surpasses that of a private pilot.) When I go to the airport and have to wait a couple hours for a plane to take off, I'm no longer frustrated. I'm happy to have more time to get things done (e.g., write, answer e-mails, or communicate with

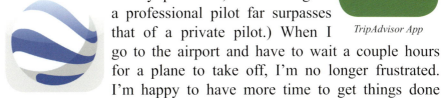

Google Earth App   *TripAdvisor App*

friends).

Even making travel arrangements is fun now. I'm able to plan entire trips using tools that are available to anyone. I use TripAdvisor to find out what the best hotels and local attractions are in the city that I'm going to visit. I use Google Earth to zoom in on the exact area where I'm staying so I have a mental picture of it before I ever leave home. I use Expedia to book all my travel—it's click, click, click, and I'm done! *(Go to the link at the end of this chapter to find out more about Google Earth, TripAdvisor and Expedia.)*

Before we continue, I want you to ask you: Is your perspective on travel warped? Do you have a degree of angst about the whole process? Are there things that bother you about it? If so, I would suggest that, like I once did, you have a weak understanding of how to navigate the system successfully so you can enjoy it from beginning to end. But don't worry! The purpose of this book is to show you how to continuously improve your travel experience, using lessons I have learned through years of being on the road.

Throughout this book, I'm going to share terms that are common in Lean manufacturing and give you examples to help you become a Lean thinker, so that you can apply the principles to every aspect of your life, including travel. Here are a few:

One-piece flow

One-piece flow means to focus on one task at a time without putting anything off or letting work accumulate. When the flight attendant hands you the customs form, don't stuff it in the pouch in the front of the seat and then later panic when the plane has landed and you have to pull it out and get it done as everyone's leaving the plane. Do it now! To be even more efficient, it helps to memorize your passport number and flight number so you don't have to jockey around trying to find the information.

Batch work

Batch work is the opposite of one-piece flow. When you say, "I'll get to that later," and you put each task on a to-do list, you create batch work for yourself. Eventually, you accumulate a whole bunch of things to do at a later time, which makes it harder to complete them. If you wait too long, you can't remember all the details, which means you must spend a whole bunch of time going back and collecting the information you had at your fingertips when you first received it. (Managing all this is over-processing.)

Single-Minute Exchange of Dies

In the Lean world, SMED means to change a die or machine out in a few minutes so that you don't have to make large batches.

Pages App

With Lean Travel, SMED requires making sure it is easy to change between tasks so that you do not put them off until a later date. For example, when I started writing this book, I was using both my computer and my iPhone to type it. However, I noticed I was regularly putting off writing, because my computer's dictation function was harder to use than the iPhone's. Dictation was easy on my iPhone but the editing was difficult because the font was very small and I don't have the best eyesight. I preferred to use the iPhone because it was easier to keep at hand and also more versatile. I could more easily switch between tasks such as answering e-mails, banging out a chapter in the book, or booking a flight reservation. The solution turned out to be simple. I increased the font size in the Pages App on my iPhone and before long, I was doing everything on the phone. Problem solved. *(Go to the link at the end of this chapter to find out more about the Pages App.)*

Standardization

By using standardized processes, you remove the burden from everything you do and make your work more productive and more effective. In this case, I standardized my work so I could use my iPhone for 98% of the processes that I perform every day as opposed to jockeying back-and-forth between the laptop and iPhone.

Muda (waste)

I mentioned the eight wastes of Lean in the introduction, and we'll talk about those more as we go along. The first and most important waste is overproduction, which is when we make too much of something. If you create excess product, it is cumbersome to manage it. Packing too much stuff for a trip is an example of overproduction when we travel. We carry so many things we really don't need and it just encumbers the entire system.

We will talk about a lot of other terms throughout the course of this book and you'll start to see how understanding Lean manufacturing and becoming a Lean thinker is highly relevant to travel. So let's get started. *(Go to the link at the end of this chapter to find out more about 2 Second Lean.)*

The One Thing:
For the love of God, understand your weaknesses and your distortions and turn them into your strength!

---

paulakers.net/lt-02

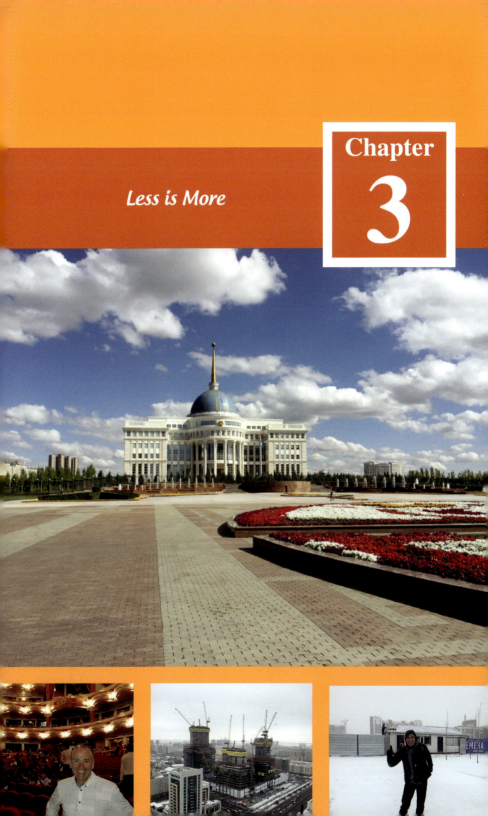

Chapter 3

Less is More

The secret to Lean Travel is this: Less is more, and lighter is better.

I remember sitting down to dinner about ten years ago with a friend of mine from the East Coast, listening to one of his travel stories. He said that when he went to China and checked into his hotel, he spent the first two hours unpacking his bags and rearranging everything inside. As he told me this, I wondered how it managed to get unarranged—wasn't it just sitting in his suitcase the whole time? He wasn't happy because he could have used those two hours to do more interesting things.

Most people encounter the same issue when they travel. They bring too much stuff, which means they have to spend a lot of time sifting through it and trying to stay organized. They end up wasting time when they could be out enjoying their destination! A much simpler solution than repacking everything would be to bring less stuff in the first place. Anderson Cooper, the world-renowned reporter, inspired me to travel lightly. He was asked in an interview how he was able to travel all over the world so effectively. He said, "The key is to travel light. I only take a few things with me and I seem to be able to manage everywhere I go."

Too many suitcases

Waste is everywhere in the travel experience, just as it is in manufacturing. If we compare the two, carrying too much stuff is like overproduction—it leads to many other problems. In a factory, when you produce too many goods, you have to manage all of your excess inventory—moving it around, finding storage space, creating a complex inventory control system, etc.—and it is all waste! When you travel with too many things, you need a bigger suitcase, which takes extra time to fill. You have to check the bag instead of carrying it onto the plane, and then you have to wait at the baggage carousel to pick it up.

Wasted human potential

The excess items lead to over-processing, motion, waiting, and some wasted human potential...yours, because now you're sitting there with herds of people waiting to get your bag and instead of writing your next book, answering an e-mail, or communicating with friends.

Over the years, I've learned a couple tricks that can help you overcome your tendency to bring too many things. First, stop packing as if you're going to have an emergency and start packing like your trip is going to go off without a hitch. If you travel with an optimistic outlook, you won't feel the need to carry every possible remedy for every possible bad situation.

Second, don't be afraid to wear the same things more than once during a trip. Most clothes can be worn multiple times without any problem. If you're worried about what people think of you, don't. Most of the time, it is highly unlikely that you will see the same people over and over again, and even if you do, other people really could care less about what you are wearing. Most people are so preoccupied with how they themselves look, they aren't paying as much attention to you as you think.

One of the best lessons I have learned while traveling is how few clothes I actually need. In the past, if I was going to be gone for five days, I would bring five days' worth of clothes. For a seven-day trip, seven days' worth. When I needed to travel for two weeks, it seemed like I was hauling everything but the kitchen sink with me. It was total insanity! I always ended up lugging around a bunch of dirty laundry too, and no one wants to do that.

If I'm in a situation where I need a couple of extra shirts because I feel like the people are going to start noticing I'm wearing the same one over and over again, I just purchase a new one. Thirty, forty bucks for a dress shirt? The convenience of lighter luggage is worth the cost, especially since I rarely need to buy new clothes.

Now, I know that a lot of women are reading this chapter right now and saying, "That's easy for you to say. You're not a woman." You know what? I've seen many women travel with suitcases as light as mine, because they know that carrying loads of stuff around is not worth it. Being free and light is easy, and makes traveling much better.

The truth is, you don't need more than five days' worth of clothes

Creative clothes drying. Whenever I need to wash my socks and they won't dry fast enough I set the hair dryer up in the sink and it creates a nice little vortex and they dry quickly over the faucet.

on almost any trip. If you're worried about the people you meet on your business trips being judgmental about your clothes, don't. I regularly deal with some very exclusive people, and no one has said anything to me yet. Your outerwear (e.g., dress shirts and pants) really shouldn't get that dirty. They can easily go two, three, even five days without being washed. I've found that the trick is to wear a lightweight nylon shirt underneath your dress shirt, which keeps the dress shirt from getting sweaty.

For me, the magic number to make things lighter is three. I take three pairs of dress socks, three undershirts, and three pairs of underwear. In addition, I take one pair of dress shoes, one pair of running shoes, and a pair of sandals—three pairs of shoes to deal with nearly any situation that could come up. I also bring five dress shirts and a pair of running socks.

One of the best ways to extend the length of your clothes is to wash them yourself. It isn't very complicated. You fill the sink with hot water, add a little shampoo (or a travel packet of laundry detergent), scrub the clothes, rinse them out, and hang them over a chair outside on the balcony. Hanging them over a lamp shade also works well because the heat from the lamp dries them out quickly. It only takes a few minutes to wash my undergarments, and I just press and iron the other stuff

Closets, chairs, and balconies are great for drying your clothes

I found the fastest way to iron my clothes was to lay them out on the bed and iron them on the sheets. It's faster, easier, and it is one less step of setting up and putting away the stupid ironing board.

Great quality and perfect for traveling with ease and care

as needed so I can look absolutely perfect. This one trick alone has allowed me to pack so much lighter than I ever dreamed. If you're not predisposed to doing your own laundry in the sink, have the hotel do it. Or, if you want to save some money, take it to a nearby laundry. There are lots of places around the world where you can get your laundry done very cheaply. For example, in Thailand, about five dollars can get a whole week's worth of laundry done. *(Go to the link at the end of this chapter to learn how to dry your clothes in the sink!)*

Certain brands of clothing are more suitable for travel than others. One of my favorites is ExOfficio, a high-quality outdoor brand. ExOfficio clothes are a little expensive ($80-$100 for a shirt, and around $80 for a pair of pants), but they are durable, lightweight, and dry quickly when wet. (The company has also invented underwear so good that some guy traveled all the way around the world with two pairs of underwear for a whole year. I carry three pairs with me.) For colder destinations, I have a Patagonia coat that is very lightweight, and it looks sharp too. It fits easily in my backpack, and keeps me warm in the coldest of climates. When I go outside in Kazakhstan and it's 20 degrees below zero, the jacket is adequate to get me to and from the car. Even if I go hiking in it, the jacket's hood provides good protection from most weather conditions I encounter. *(Go to the link at the end of this chapter*

Top Image: *I am dressed up and ready to do battle with his team in Kazakhstan. I have Deep respect for the people that can work in this climate and not complained once.*

Bottom Image: *Ready to work in 40° below zero weather in Kazakhstan. Notice the Russian felt boots. Nobody will ever beat the Russians in a war as long as they have these boots to keep them warm.*

to see Paul's skiing adventure in Kazakhstan.)

The one problem with these brands is that they cost more than you might typically spend on clothing. This is where you have to make an important choice: Would you rather spend $250 (the price of the Patagonia jacket) and have a high-quality, portable product that's going to last, or would you rather spend less money, take two or three of something, and have to manage them for the entire trip? If you want to simplify your travel, you choose the first option.

While clothes are a major contributor to over-packing, they are not the only one. Travelers often carry too much electronic gear, especially cameras. We tell ourselves we need every type of camera to get the "perfect" shot. I completely understand—if anybody likes to carry a lot of camera gear, it's me. I am a photographer, a videographer, and a drone enthusiast. In the past, everywhere I went I would bring my video camera, my FastCam (action camera), an iPhone camera, and my 35mm camera. My bags were heavy! *(Go to the link at the end of this chapter to find out more about FastCap's FastCam.)*

Now, because camera technology has advanced so far, I get away with just bringing my iPhone for snapshots and my ground-based video work. The only other camera I take with me is my drone (DJI Phantom4), because it allows me to get some spectacular footage of the places I visit. Carrying a drone can be a challenge, but it is manageable, too. I used to bring a large specialized backpack for it, but once I figured out how to eliminate the waste of packing, I could fit it inside a normal backpack along with the rest of my stuff. Now I only bring one backpack and a carry-on suitcase with me. *(Go to the link at the end of this chapter to find out more about the DJ's Phantom 4.)*

Whenever you travel, think "less is more." Think about eliminating waste when you pack and use the tips above to extend the use of what you carry with you. If you do, your satisfaction will be that much greater and you'll be surprised how little you need. Give it a try, and you'll be shocked at how much simpler, smoother, and more rewarding your travel will be.

> **The One Thing:**
> *Stop planning for an emergency and start planning for success.*

paulakers.net/lt-03

Chapter 4

Debacle in Dubai

The magic is having just two pieces of luggage. A roll-on suitcase and a backpack

Because I've learned to travel with fewer things, no matter where I'm traveling or how long I'm going to be away, I only bring a backpack and a roll-around suitcase to carry onto the plane. With only those two pieces of luggage to manage, life on the road is quite simple. But the minute I add anything to that, trouble seems to follow closely behind, at least when it comes to luggage.

My first bag debacle happened when my wife and I went on a safari in South Africa. While there, we found a store that had some beautiful hand-embroidered pillowcases and a lot of other unique items that Leanne wanted to buy as Christmas gifts for her family. By the time she finished shopping, we had somewhere around a thousand dollars' worth of gifts in a nicely-packed gift bag. It was great to get some of our Christmas shopping done, but it also gave us an extra bag to carry the rest of the trip.

While traveling back to the States, Leanne managed the extra bag from South Africa to Dubai. In Dubai, I offered to carry it around the airport while we waited for our next flight. When it was time to board the plane, I set the bag down and reached into my pocket to get my passport and ticket out. Because I was not used to carrying the third bag, it slipped my mind that I had set it down, and I walked to the plane without it. *(Go to the link at the end of this chapter to check out Paul & Leanne's experience in Dubai.)*

A few minutes later, as I was putting my things in the overhead bin, I realized what I'd done. I ran back up the gangway as fast as I could, but by the time I got to the terminal, the bag was gone. No one had seen it.

I felt terrible. It wasn't just that I had lost the bag. It was that I had lost the bag my wife had entrusted to me that was full of Christmas gifts. Breaking her trust hurt much worse than losing the actual objects.

Unfortunately, I did something similar three years later. I was at the Madrid airport looking for a gift for my friend Assel, who I was going to visit in Portugal. I saw a store that sold these fantastic bottles of olive oil. Assel likes to cook, and the oil would be the perfect gift. I told the man helping me that I would like to buy some but security probably would not let it on the plane. He said, "It's no problem. We can pack it special and they will let you carry it on." I explained that Assel would also need to be able to check it on the airplane when she returned home to Belgium. Once again, he reassured me: "As long as she doesn't open it, they will let it through security and she won't have any problems."

With the special packaging, the bottles wouldn't fit in my backpack, so I had to carry them in a separate bag. That almost convinced me to not get the oil, but I really wanted to bring Assel a gift, so I bought it anyway... I should have known better.

"Paul, how could you lose my olive oil?"

It didn't take more than ten minutes before I lost that olive oil. I went over to the gate, sat down, and put it on the floor next to my suitcase. Just like in Dubai, when they called for the final boarding, I sprang to my feet, grabbed my luggage and walked off, leaving the olive oil right next to the chair where I was sitting. This time, I didn't even make it to the plane before I realized something was missing. I turned around and ran back up the gangway as fast as I could, but the oil was gone. I couldn't believe it. No more than four or five minutes had transpired and the bag was already gone. I chastised myself: Paul, you've learned your lesson: Three bags is a curse.

The two debacles hammered home the idea for me that less is more. When I had only two bags that were always linked together, it was very difficult to lose either of them. But the minute there was a third bag involved, the potential to lose something increased exponentially. I learned that if you're going to buy something when you travel, it should fit in your suitcase or your backpack. Today, my single roll-around suitcase plus the backpack that fits over the handle is my travel profile. This makes it much easier to negotiate airports, airplanes, hotels, and rental cars. It is compact, easy to monitor, and nothing gets left behind.

If you remember earlier, I said people often look at me and marvel, "Paul how do you travel with so little and do it so gracefully?" The answer is simple: I follow the principle that "less is more" and stick to it.

Another thing that helps me travel more smoothly is an understanding of source management. My great friend, Ritsuo Shingo, former president of Toyota China, explained source management this way: If you have a mighty river and you want to change its direction, trying to divert it at the mouth of the river where it meets the ocean would be very difficult. At that point, the river is big and wide and often the current is powerful. If, however, you go up into the mountains to where the river is just a small trickle of water, it is very easy just to move your foot a little to the left or the right and change the direction of the entire river. *(Go to the link at the end of this chapter to find out more about Ritsuo Shingo.)*

My good friend, Ritsuo Shingo

Don't solve problems at the mouth of the river. Go to the head waters, the source.

With source management, you look hard at your problems and go right to the place where they are created. In the example of losing the extra bag, what is truly the source of the problem? At the most fundamental level, it's the notion that possessions make people happy.

Travelers tend to buy little tchotchkes (knickknacks) and bring them home because we think people will really enjoy and appreciate them. I'm sure there are some who do, but most people just end up with shelves full of unwanted junk because people push these things on them.

Understanding "push" and "pull" is important in this context. In Lean manufacturing, we always want the customer to create demand (i.e., "pull") for a product. This eliminates overproduction, which causes all kinds of other problems. Likewise, when traveling, we never want to push anything on anyone. The minute we push, the waste stream goes crazy. Whether we are pushing these tchotchke gifts on our friends and family, or the airlines are pushing bad food on us when we are flying, so much of this stuff gets wasted. Love pull and hate push!

The people you want to buy all these gifts for would be more pleased with regularly hearing from you, receiving a thoughtful picture via e-mail or posted on Facebook, or following effective real-time journalizing of your trips so they could travel virtually with you and learn from your experiences.

In other words, connecting with people is more important than piling things on them. For me, the source of the excess luggage problem is a misunderstanding of what is really important to people. When you reduce your material desires, you free yourself to connect with others on a more personal level. If you make it your top priority to connect and communicate with people and not load them up with junk, you can lessen the management burden of your travel, too.

Pursuing minimalism and keeping things as simple as possible has become an obsession for me. I can't count how many times I've traveled with people who bought an extra suitcase to haul their purchases home from a long trip. They spend more money on a suitcase they don't need, and have to manage that extra suitcase throughout the duration of their trip. It costs more money to get the cheap crap home because they have to pay for an extra suitcase. Finally, the person receiving the gift has to take care of that gift, and it clutters up their life until they get rid of it. Waste, waste, waste!

The power of simplicity extends beyond travel, too. Recently, my assistant Lori and her husband sold their big house, got rid of 80% of their stuff, and moved into a small two-bedroom condominium. I asked her how she liked it, and her reply circles around in my mind every day: "I love it. Every weekend, Keith and I decide what we're going to go do instead of staying home and working on our house, cleaning, or doing projects. We're actually enjoying life!"

I may seem cynical about giving gifts, but I have seen what people actually do with all these things. The vast majority of them are not appreciated, and all of this stuff really adds up. A few years back I received a very insightful e-mail from one of the listeners to my show, The American Innovator:

Paul at the studio for his podcast, The American Innovator

Paul,

Have you ever thought about the real cost of poor quality? We fill stores with low-quality products that people buy because they are less expensive. The product gets used three or four times and they often underperform or flat-out fail. Then we relegate this stuff to our closets, garages, and storage lockers. We build bigger houses with more storage that cost more to heat and maintain. Our property taxes go up, the time it takes to clean them goes up, and the very thing we all desperately want—happiness—is sucked up by the addition of managing all our stuff. Once a year we clean house and throw and give away all that stuff that we thought would make us happy.

The vast majority of the stuff ends up in landfills that we have to manage for the next forty or fifty years with more big heavy equipment and scientific testing to make sure we're not contaminating the environment. If that's not enough, then we have to consider the cost of all materials and resources that went into making that stuff in the first place. Then the cost of transporting low-quality products to the stores then to our homes, to Goodwill, and then to the landfill. The entire real cost of a low-quality product versus an expensive product is staggering. In most cases, you could purchase a high-quality product for a fraction of the cost of a low-quality one. *(Go to the link at the end of this chapter to find out more about The American Innovator Podcast.)*

What an insightful e-mail! His words helped me see how I confused accumulating material goods with spiritual satisfaction. Thankfully, I'm learning to think differently.

It is much better to give people something that will have lasting meaning. For me, that something has been the stories I tell in my videos that I share to inspire others to explore the world for themselves and the books that I write.

Journey around Portugal with Assel

The best example I can think of comes from something I did for Assel when I visited her in Portugal after I forgot the olive oil. Over four days, she took me around and showed me the sights and sounds of this amazing country. Unbeknownst to her, the entire time I was discreetly taking short video clips of what we had been doing using my iPhone. In the evenings, I put the clips together to create a video highlighting the wonderful things we experienced together. The last thing I needed was the right music.

On the last day of the trip Assel came downstairs to my bedroom, knocked on the door, and sat on the edge of my bed with her computer. She asked me if I had heard Ed Sheeran's song "Photograph." She clicked on her laptop and played me the video. I began to cry because it was the most beautiful song I had ever heard. The video depicted Ed's life from when he was a baby through his rise to stardom, using the pictures and video clips his parents had taken over the years. Clearly, this song was very meaningful to Assel, and I thought that if I put the photographs from our trip to this song, it could really highlight how special the four days had been for both of us.

I finished making the photo/video montage and gave it to Assel right before I left. Needless to say, it was emotional and meaningful for her. To this day we still talk about it. It so perfectly captured a moment that neither of us ever wanted to forget. Sure, the olive oil would have been a nice gift, but the four minute music video is something that will help us cherish those memories for the rest of our lives. There was no package to open, there was no waste—just a simple click on her phone and the music began to play.

Be thoughtful when you travel, and avoid your own bag debacles by limiting what you bring back with you. Don't let your presence and your ability to emotionally connect with people on a daily basis be masked with materialism. You will simplify not only your life, but your travel as well.

> **The One Thing:**
> Go to the source of the problem. Solve problems at the source and your burdens will be light...less is more.

paulakers.net/lt-04

Chapter 5

Just-In-Time Travel

Most people believe that to get good flights and hotels at reasonable prices you have to plan way in advance. I always used to think that too, but in the last year, I've learned it's not always the case. If you're planning a great big vacation for your family, you probably need some predictability in how you plan and organize your trip. But if you are spontaneously traveling all over the world, you have to frequently change and rearrange your travel plans. For people with this type of lifestyle, just-in-time travel is the way to go.

With just-in-time travel, you arrange your travel as you go, instead of planning it out far in advance. Now I rarely book hotel arrangements more than two weeks in advance, and I frequently even book them on the same day. You get the best deals at the last minute because a day, a week, or sometimes two weeks in advance, hotels look at their reservations and calculate when they will have extra rooms to fill. They contact sites like Expedia and offer them discounts to entice flexible customers (like me) to book with them. I am shocked when I reflect back on all the consternation I put myself through thinking I needed to book in advance to get a room. By making reservations so early, all I did was make my schedule less adaptable to my ever-changing needs.

The same principle applies to flight reservations. In the past I always thought I needed to book way ahead of time or I wouldn't get a seat. Not anymore. People's ability to access information and schedule flights online is much more fluid, so fewer travelers reserve their flights way in advance and planes are not booked full as early as they were in the past. My general rule of thumb for making flight reservations is to book them a week before I'm ready to go. For international flights, I will book two to three weeks in advance, but even that's not always necessary. I've seen amazing discounts on fares the same week as the flight. In fact, I recently flew to Germany, and one week before the flight, I visited Expedia and found a flight on Condor Airlines for $800 (round-trip!). These kind of deals exist just-in-time and at the last minute. You just have to be a little patient and understand the system.

Use Expedia and other Apps to get the best deals

Technology has made planning travel so much better, and Expedia has become my go-to resource for almost all travel bookings. I've often booked flights and hotels in under 60 seconds. I find the hotel, find the flight, and then it's click, click, done. The bookings are automatically added to my list of trips and I can review them anytime I want. I used to monitor all my reservations with an app called TripIt, but frankly, Expedia's travel log of trips is so effective and efficient that I don't use TripIt much anymore.

Expedia App

When I'm booking an international flight and I'm not familiar with the local carriers at my destination, I use an App called Skyscanner. A good friend of mine in Spain showed it to me. It scans all the airlines, including several (e.g., Southwest, Ryanair, and Eurowings) that might not show up in search engines like Expedia or KAYAK because they don't work with travel websites. Skyscanner allows you to know every possible flight available, no matter how small or obscure the airline is. Once you determine that a particular carrier has the flight you need, you can go directly to the carrier's website and book it if it is not available through Expedia.

Skyscanner App
The best times saving app ever! Gives you the big picture, fast and easy.

The App from Alaska Airlines is also crazy good. Alaska Airlines flights do show up on Expedia, but sometimes I find it very convenient just to book directly with Alaska. The nice thing about these apps is they store my credit card information, so all I have to do is enter my security code and I'm done with the reservation. Because I can make my own travel plans so quickly from my iPhone, I never have to explain them to an assistant, which saves me a lot of time and headaches from miscommunications. (In Lean terms, giving the assistant the explanation would be considered over-processing.) *(Go to the link at the end of this chapter to find out more about the Expedia, Sckyscanner, Alaska Airlines, and TripAdvisor Apps.)*

Alaska Airline App

Another benefit of just-in-time travel is that if my plans change, I pay fewer cancellation fees than I used to. Expedia has an exceptional feature that if you book a flight, you have 24 hours to cancel it. Often,

I'll think I've found the perfect flight and book it, but over the course of the next 24 hours I decide it isn't going to work out. With three clicks, the reservation is cancelled and I am done, without any hassle.

Sometimes I'll go to six or seven countries on a single trip, and I used to worry about the ability of a website to handle multiple destinations. However, because the Expedia App does not allow you to book multiple destinations (the company's website does), I had to figure out another way to make plans. As I did, I learned a little secret: You don't want to do multiple destinations in the same booking, because if anything changes, you screw up the entire reservation.

When I recently went to Expedia to make a couple changes on a multi-city reservation, they told me it would cost $150 for each change. It was a nightmare. That's when it clicked—why was I creating this big batch of flights? Why not do one-piece flow instead? In Lean manufacturing, one-piece flow has been shown to be more efficient than batch processing. When making flight plans now, I apply one-piece flow by only booking one leg at a time. That way, if my schedule changes at the last minute, I only have to rebook the one leg and pay one penalty fee.

Side note: *The superior efficiency of one-piece flow is counterintuitive and most people don't believe it until they see it in action. The best way to contrast the two methods is to show people a three-minute demonstration of manufacturing paper airplanes. You start with two groups. One group makes airplanes by performing each fold separately on ten sheets of paper before moving on to the next step in the process (batch processing). The other group makes complete airplanes from each piece of paper before moving on to the next one*

Jayme and I did an experiment. We both built paper airplanes for 5 minutes. Jayme did hers as one piece flow; one airplane from start to finish. I built my planes in a batch: I put one the wings, then the landing gears, and then the electronics passing incompleted planes from station to station. In 5 minutes Jayme had completed 7 airplanes ready to ship and collect payment on. I had zero completed and a whole bunch of work in process.

(one-piece flow). At the end of three minutes, the different results are staggering. The group using batch processing has maybe one or two planes done, a bunch of work in process, and a bunch of materials inventory that they haven't yet touched. The team using one-piece-flow usually has eight to ten airplanes completed, tested, and ready to fly. Batch work is less efficient because you have to manage all the parts, repeatedly stacking them, moving them and revisiting them. You want to avoid the same thing when booking a reservation or planning your travel. Making them one at a time is the simplest way to do this. *(Go to the link at the end of this chapter to see who wins the paper airplane challenge. One-piece flow vs. Batch work!)*

Additionally, if you book each leg completely independently, it is easier to organize your travel schedule. When you look at your trips menu on the Expedia app, you can see all the different destinations. If you need to modify one, you just select the city you're flying to and modify only that one.

Loewe introducing Ctrip

You could argue that it is easier to let the travel companies figure out all the connection times for you, but frankly, it's easy to do by opening multiple tabs in your browser and clicking back and forth to check the connection times. There's nothing hard about figuring out connections, especially if you're not checking bags that have to be shuttled from airline to airline. When you check bags you add complexity and the potential for defects, as we already discussed. If you travel with multiple carriers, you set yourself up for problems. Sometimes when you make a connection, an airline will check your bags through to another, but most of the time, if you switch carriers you'll have to go outside of security, retrieve your bag from the luggage claim, and go back through the screening process. It's better to just carry it onto each plane yourself and avoid that ritual. *(Go to the link at the end of this chapter to find out more about the Ctrip App.)*

Ctrip App

Be curious and continually improve

This point of this book is to teach you about Lean Travel, which looks to eliminate waste in all processes through continuous improvement. We must always be looking for ways to improve. The key is to be a little curious—if you ask questions, you'll be shocked how much you learn. Wherever I'm traveling, I'm always talking to the people that I meet and asking them to share their tricks to traveling more efficiently. Loewe, a friend of mine who lives in China, told me about an app the Chinese use, called Ctrip. It is similar to Expedia and I use it all the time when I'm traveling in Asia because I can get better deals and more options than Expedia offers in those countries.

One of my favorite examples of just-in-time travel is getting upgraded to business class. You can buy the upgrade at the list price when you book your flight, or you can wait until you get to the gate or even on board the plane and ask if upgrades are available. When you wait, you'll pay a fraction of the cost.

If I am taking an international flight that is eight hours or longer, I really try to get upgraded to business class. I get a lot more done when I have more room to comfortably spread out, then leads to being more rested for work or play once I arrive. To improve my chances of getting the upgrade, I try to show up to the airport three or four hours before my flight. International flights typically open four hours before the takeoff time, and if you're the first one in line, you'll have the best opportunity to check the price of the business class upgrade. The airlines will give you the best deal if you book the flight directly with them, but even if you don't, upgrades are often still available, so always ask. If you don't like the quoted price, try again.

Persistence will take you far

As I type these words, I'm at 36,000 feet en route from Santiago, Chile, to Easter Island. I sit here fully stretched-out in the emergency exit row on a beautiful 787 Dreamliner with more room than they have in first class. How did I pull this off? Persistence and experience!

This is how it happened: My wife and I got to the check-in counter early and asked if the emergency exit row was available. The ticket agent said no, they were all full, so we asked for business class upgrades instead. She said they were $2,500 each, and we would have to go upstairs to the ticket purchase counter if we wanted to buy them. We ran upstairs, and the agents there confirmed they were $2,500 each. Unwilling to pay so much, we asked again for exit row seats and were told to go to a different counter where someone might be able to help us. (The first woman at the check-in counter had told us we were not eligible for the emergency exit row because we did not speak Spanish. Being an experienced traveler, I knew it was rare they use that criteria.) I asked again at the third counter as nicely as I could, throwing in as many Spanish words as I knew. The agent was very accommodating and before long he was tearing up our original tickets (which were terrible) and handing us two emergency exit row seats that were fantastic. Score!!!

Plenty of leg room in Emergency Exit seating

As we walked away, I thought we should try to get exit row seats secured for the return trip three days later, so we circled back to the same counter and asked if we could book the same seats for the return flight. Shockingly, the answer was different yet again! This time, the agent said we could not book them, and even if we could, it would cost extra money. (This was the same man who gave us two upgrade tickets in under four minutes and never mentioned a word about charging us anything.) He went on to say you could only do it 48 hours before the flight and you had to do it online. I asked him to please try one more time. He went into his computer, and 60 seconds later he booked the same seats for our return flight, with no extra charge. The moral of the story is to always be persistent.

To give yourself the best chance to improve your seats on a flight, follow these steps:

1. Ask for the emergency exit row because those seats disappear quickly. If one is available, you want the agent to immediately secure it for you in the system. Do not distract the agent with any activity other than reserving you the exit row seat. I have seen those seats disappear right in front of me because the agent was busy with something else.

2. If you cannot get an exit row seat, ask for the availability of a business class upgrade. If the price is reasonable (my threshold is $800), make a decision before moving to step 3.

3. If you strike out at the initial check-in counter, proceed to the gate and ask the same questions again. You would be surprised how many times you will get a totally different answer.

4. If the answer you receive at the gate is not favorable, make sure you're the last one on the plane and ask the flight attendant as you board. Many times I've been quoted $2,000 at the check-in counter and then paid $500 for business class upgrade on the plane.

5. If you strike out three times in a row, never fear. Peruse the plane seats as you board and see if you can get a seat with an open one next to it or an exit seat that is not taken.

Only once in the last three years did one of these strategies not work out for me.

Persistence pays when it comes to booking hotels too. One of my favorite places in the world is Phuket, Thailand. I can go on and on about Phuket—the beautiful beaches, warm water, great food, reasonable prices, and friendly people. Every time I go there I try to find a place that is more

Exploring Phuket scooter style.

affordable with a location that is more desirable. The last time I went, I was practicing just-in-time travel, so I only booked a hotel for one night (of a ten-day visit). When I looked at it online, it seemed like a nice place, but not the kind of place where I wanted to spend a week and half. (My first night's stay confirmed that.)

The next morning I woke up, rented a scooter for five bucks, and  drove around to ten different hotels that, according to Expedia and TripAdvisor, also offered great value. After looking at nine of them, I was a little discouraged. Phuket was very busy this time of year, so there wasn't much available. Was my just-in-time system going to fail me? No. Just because most people were booked up didn't mean everyone was booked. Besides, the hotel where I was staying had rooms available if there were no other options.

Ask questions! Find out from the locals where to go and explore.

Finally, I pulled up to the tenth hotel and took a look. It was spectacular, with huge suite rooms, beautiful furnishings, elegant bathrooms, and five pools (and heavily discounted at only $60 a night, compared to the normal rate of $150-$180 per night). To top it off, nobody was there! Just-in-time travel, plus a little persistence paid off for me—big time. *(Go to the link at the end of this chapter to check out Paul's scooter ride through Phuket.)*

Orientation

Nestled neatly within the concept of just-in-time travel is the concept of the orientation day. When I'm traveling to a new location and I know I'm going to be there for three to five days, I often don't book anything until I take some time and become oriented with my surroundings. I call this my orientation day. Similar to how I checked out several hotels in Phuket, I use the first day of a trip to discover the ins and outs of a new destination.

Exploring the foods of Phuket.

For example, as we flew to Easter Island, I talked to the flight attendant, Catalina, and she told me all kinds of great things to do and see. She had been to Easter Island five times and had collected lots of local knowledge. (Catalina's insights weren't quite my first exposure to Easter Island—a week earlier, I had begun watching YouTube videos online to understand what the island was all about.) She even invited our group to a barbecue that the flight team was having at one of the best beaches on the island (talk about having the inside track!). Shortly after landing, we rented a quad so we could track all over the island and get the layout of the land. Traversing the island, talking to the locals about the best things to do, I ended up with lots of great ideas.

Another trick for getting oriented is to not be too quick to commit to a certain hotel or restaurant. Take a look around before you set in stone what you're going to do. In the past, when choosing a restaurant we would stop in at any restaurant that looked good, with mixed results. Now we do something called restaurant hopping. We choose a restaurant, order one or two hors d'oeuvres or a main course and a glass of wine, and then move to the next restaurant. During the whole evening you can visit two or three restaurants easily and really get oriented as to what the local food is all about.

I learned this concept from my friends Cindy and Gordon when we were in Dubai. We went to four restaurants in one night and we had a ball tasting all the different foods. At each one, we ordered a few small dishes to sample instead of a full meal. At one point we even had a restaurant bringing the food to us at another restaurant. We were laughing so hard and having such a great time. Everyone thought we were a little crazy but they enjoyed how much fun we were having. We basically experienced four days of eating in one night, so we knew what was good when we went out to eat the next day.

Cindy and Gordon taught us the art of grazing at restaurants. Only eating a little at each restaurant.

On Easter Island, my wife and I did the same thing. We ordered ceviche at multiple restaurants to find out who had the best food in town. Surprisingly, the restaurateurs loved the concept and supported it completely. We were very upfront and honest with them about what we were doing, and it actually made them want to perform at a higher level because they knew we were comparing them to everyone else on the same night.

Go for it

When we returned from Easter Island to Santiago, our plane was once again a beautiful 787 Dreamliner. I was the last one to get on the plane, and as I passed by the cockpit, I asked if I could go into the front office (cockpit) and take a look. Before long the pilots waved me forward and I was shooting a video and taking pictures in the front of the 787 Dreamliner. I repeated

Paul in the front office with the 787 Dreamliner Pilots.

this same experience when I was on the Emirates Airline Airbus 380 en route from New York to Dubai. People always shake their heads at me and say, "Paul how do you have all these amazing experiences?" It's simple, if you are willing to do these five things:

Continuously improve.
Be intensely curious.
Experiment without fear.
Ask if something is possible.
Do not be afraid to look foolish.

When it is your turn to travel, don't stress if you do not have all your arrangements made weeks in advance. Relax and think about how you can incorporate these five suggestions into your preparations. There are always deals out there so you don't really need to worry about booking everything way in advance anymore. In addition, you often get a much better price at the last minute than if you book something two or three months in advance. The tools are there for you to rent a car, reserve a flight, choose a hotel, find the best restaurants, or anything else you want to do, in just a few minutes' time. Take advantage of them.

Remember, travel is a process that can be enhanced and improved like anything else. I'm constantly tweaking and perfecting the travel process to make my travel more effective and enjoyable, and I do it in a very deliberate fashion. If you can learn to be fully aware of the process and identify the waste or clunky mechanics of every travel process, you will end up improving your life experiences exponentially. Who doesn't want that! *(Go to the link at the end of this chapter to see Paul run around the world!)*

The One Thing:
Just-In-Time travel is king, and flexibility is queen. So locking things down way in advance is not necessarily to your advantage.

---

paulakers.net/lt-05

Chapter 6

Always

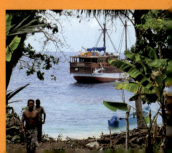

This is a fun chapter for me, because it talks about principles that will consistently remove the struggles of travel and make it more predictable and enjoyable.

1. Always turn around and look back as you walk away from where you have been sitting.

I can't tell you the number of times I've left something sitting on the seat or the floor behind me. This is one of the most important processes you must consistently perform, regardless of where you are and what you're doing. Always turn around and glance at the place you just walked away from to make sure you didn't leave your wallet on the counter, your water bottle in the chair, or that your Bose ear buds didn't fall on the floor. This is my top Lean Travel principle.

2. Always carry things in the same place.

Remember the phrase "a place for everything and everything in its place." Make sure that you always put your headsets, your glasses, your electronics, your passport, or anything else you're using in its assigned pocket. This will eliminate enormous amounts of wasted time searching for your stuff, and you will lose fewer things because you know to always scan their specific places to make sure you have them. It will take you less time to unpack in the hotel room and less time to repack when you leave.

3. Always give your smile first.

If you were born with a smile on your face, you will love giving that smile to people as you travel around the world. Greet everybody you encounter with it. When you travel, you encounter many people who are out there serving you and helping you. You should be grateful in your heart that they're willing to do this and you should start off the relationship by treating them with a huge smile.

Win the world with your smile.

4. Always hand your passport to customs officials right-side up with your ticket inside.

Everything is a process, including boarding the plane and going through security. Make the process work more smoothly for you; don't make people struggle to clear you through the gate, security, or customs. When you properly orient your paperwork, people will appreciate your extra effort.

Always hand your passport and documents correctly oriented to the person inspecting them and greet them with a smile. You'll be shocked how much better the experience will be.

If I can't get the emergency exit seat assigned I generally get it by being the last one on the plane.

5. Always be the last one on the plane (well, almost always!).

You will read an example of why you should do this in Chapter 7, so rather than explain it all here, I'll let you wait a few pages. For now, just recognize that it can be very beneficial to board at the last minute.

6. Always sit or stand close to the door on a bus.

This is particularly important when you're on the rental car bus. It is so important to be positioned near the door, so that you're the first one off when it opens. The line for picking up rental cars can be a nightmare. There are great rental car agencies out there—Enterprise is one—but there are times when you have to use other companies who are less efficient. Be the first person off the bus and you will save yourself a lot of waiting in line. The same thing goes when you're getting off the plane and boarding a bus to take you to the terminal.

Always be the last one on the bus so you're the first one off the bus to get in line for customs or at the rental car counter.

-55-

7. Always put your overhead luggage above you or in front of you.
As you're going down the aisle to get on the plane you should look at the overhead compartment and consider putting your bag in a position in front of where you're sitting. Why? If you get to your seat and you have to put your bag behind you because the overhead storage is full, when it comes time to deplane you will need to wait for everyone else to get off before you can go back to retrieve your bag. I have often put my bags in the overhead compartments in first class when I can see the rest of the plane's storage is looking full.

Always put your carry-on in the overhead bin in front of your seat.

8. Always look to help others with their overhead bags.
If everyone would just help the people around them get their bags down from the overhead storage, particularly people who are smaller and don't have the strength to easily lift them down, the time it takes to deplane the aircraft would be cut in half. If you ever want to observe waste, just watch how inefficiently people deplane an aircraft.

9. Always tell the flight attendants what great service they have provided.
How would you like to be stuck in an aluminum tube for 30% of your life? These people work hard to make your flight enjoyable and you should go out of your way to always have an attitude of gratitude, particularly when you're exiting the plane.

10. Always tell the pilots what a great landing they made.
As a pilot, I can tell you that one of the greatest feelings is when your passengers tell you, "Wow, that was a nice landing." In the aviation world, they say any landing you walk away from is a good landing, so technically, if you're alive and well (regardless of how rough the landing seemed), the pilots did a great job. Let them know!

11. Always take out your earphones as the flight attendant approaches.

I have a friend, Barb, who is a flight attendant, and she gave me a lot of great advice about how to be a good traveler. One of her pet peeves is people who leave their earphones in their ears when she is asking them what they want to drink. Often, she has to repeat herself several times, which hampers her ability to serve all passengers efficiently. All we need to do is be a little mindful as they approach and pull our earphones out so they don't have to repeat themselves. Do unto others as you would want them to do to you. *(Go to the link at the end of this chapter to see a head phone storage tip.)*

12. Always leave the bathroom on the plane cleaner then you found it.

I don't know anybody who likes to walk into a dirty public restroom. Leave the bathroom a little bit better than you found it; pick up the paper off the floor, and drain and wash the sink out. You will be a better person deep inside of you if you do. If everyone in the world just thought this way, can you imagine how much more pleasant our lives would be?

Leave it better than you found it.

13. Always check in early and carry the confirmation number with you on your phone.

It's not always possible, but make it your routine to copy and paste your confirmation number into your calendar and into the online check-in system. This way, you avoid mistakes and the inconvenience of going through hundreds of e-mails to find your confirmation number. If you're running late, just go straight to security. I create a screenshot of my boarding pass on my iPhone by holding down the home button and the on/off button at the same time. The screenshot gets stored with my photos. I show the screen shot when I'm checking in and it works perfectly. I don't even need the electronic boarding pass to get on the plane.

14. Always bring your own thermos.

I always travel with my stainless-steel Starbucks coffee mug. It's super convenient. My drinks stay hot and I've always got water, coffee or tea to keep hydrated. (An added bonus: I can't tell you the number of times people have complimented me on how beautiful my thermos is. I didn't just buy a thermos—I bought a beautiful thermos that not only makes me feel good when I look at it, but it makes me want to drink more because it's so stunning in the way it was crafted.) I sometimes laugh at all the environmentalists that are so concerned about all the plastic and waste that is generated from water bottles and paper coffee cups. The whole problem could be solved with a simple campaign to "get personal" and reuse your own drink container. If everyone did this one simple thing, all the packaging waste eliminated would be staggering. So go buy the highest-quality, sexiest drink container you can find, hydrate your body, and save the earth!

I bought this beautiful quality Starbucks thermos in Singapore and I take it with me everywhere I go. It's slim and beautiful and it reminds me of exactly how I want to look the rest of my life. Quality, quality, quality!

15. Always keep your passport and wallet in the same pocket.

Throughout this book, I have used the word "routine" in place of "discipline." This is deliberate. I learned this concept from *What Makes Olga Run?*, a book about Olga Kotelko, a ninety-something-year-old Canadian woman who is in excellent condition and still participates in track and field at a very high level. Kotelko's routines, not her discipline, have kept her in such great shape. As the author, Bruce Grierson, so keenly observed, "Routines remove the vagary of discipline." Don't say to yourself that you need to

"What Makes Olga Run?"

remember to put your passport and wallet in the same pocket all the time; rather, make it your routine. That way, you are never saddled with the inconvenience of misplacing or losing those important items, and you can always retrieve them fast and easy.) Never rely on discipline to maintain exceptional habits; it is better to develop strong routines. *(Go to the link at the end of this chapter to find out What makes Olga Run.)*

16. Always carry a pen with you for filling out customs forms.
I spent a good part of my life stressing out when custom forms were handed out because I didn't have something to write with. Now, I always keep a cheap, lightweight pen in my backpack for filling them out.

I can't believe how much this simple thing has streamlined the travel process for me. In addition, I memorized my passport number, which makes filling out those forms that much easier.

Another trick with customs forms is to know the name of the hotel where you are staying, information that is often requested on the forms. If you don't remember, don't stress out. Customs officials rarely care what the name of the hotel is. I usually just call it something to do with the area where I'm traveling. For example, if I'm going to Baja, I write down the Baja Hotel. If I'm in Astana, Kazakhstan, I write down the "Hilton in Astana." Customs officials have not questioned me about this even once. (Don't let me get started about the waste that these documents create in the world. Somewhere there must be rooms filled with billions of these forms from countries all over the world. You would think at some point they would digitize them; we are living in the twenty-first century.)

17. Always fill out the customs forms as soon as you get it on the plane. Remember, one of the main tenets of Lean is to not create batch work, piles, or a to-do-later box. Great Lean processes allow you to do everything just in time as the demand is received. Don't wait on anything; take care of it right at that moment. If you fill out the customs forms right away, you can peacefully rest for the duration of your flight. Procrastination is the friend to failure, chaos, and a whole host of other things that will reduce the quality of your life. Avoid it.

Don't put things in the queue, do everything right away.

18. Always get your visas in advance.
The truth is, you can travel almost anywhere in the world, get off the plane, and get an emergency visa at the airport. However, acquiring a visa after you land, when you are tired, hungry, and ready to do something besides wait in line can be a real drag. For me, it's worth paying a little extra money to get pre-approved and secure the visa ahead of time. It's one less thing I have to contend with when I'm traveling in a foreign country.

19. Always take an apple and nuts as a snack.
It would be nearly impossible for you to walk up to me and not find an apple or nuts in my backpack. I love life, so I take my health seriously and refuse to eat junk food because I wasn't prepared enough to bring a healthy snack. I only fuel this Ferrari (my body) with the best quality food!

20. Always carry your luggage onto the plane.
There are two concepts here that are important to note: First, if you need to check your bag, you are bringing too much stuff; and second, maintaining control of your luggage is a surefire way to maintain control of your travel. There's nothing worse than losing a bag! Once, when my wife and I were traveling to Aspen, I had all my ski gear in my bag. I wasn't planning to

check it, but the overhead compartments were full so I had no choice but to check it at the gate. When we got off the plane, somebody grabbed my bag that was sitting on the jetway and I grabbed theirs. At the hotel, I opened up my suitcase and realized that none of the things inside were mine. We had very similar cases, so the mistake was easily understandable, but that didn't solve the problem. As a result, we had to purchase thousands of dollars' worth of ski clothes at a very expensive store in Aspen. I've since added some kind of a mark on all my luggage (eg., an orange ribbon, a sticker, etc.) that allows me to quickly identify my luggage from everyone else's. Now it would be almost impossible to grab the wrong bag, especially since I rarely check it.

21. Always arrive one hour before your flight.
I once had a young girl ask me what the key to life was, and I told her it was to understand the power of margin! Having a little margin, or, in this case, a little extra time or resources at your disposal will come in very handy (see #38). This particularly applies to the aviation industry. You never know what the check-in lines are going to look like or how slow security will be—believe me, they can both really surprise you.

Someone once told me that the real adventure starts when everything goes wrong, but I don't ascribe to that at all. The real adventure starts when things go as planned and you have the flexibility to do whatever you want to do. Arriving early at the airport helps you ensure that happens.

22. Always go to your gate and confirm it is the correct one before you go shopping or to the lounge.
In the past, if I had an hour before I needed to get to the gate, I would go get a cup of coffee or head for the airport lounge. Never again. I've had gates change on me and have had to

No shopping! Confirm your gate first.

rush to an entirely different terminal to get to the new gate in time for my flight. Large airports like Dallas/Fort Worth or Chicago's O'Hare can really throw some curveballs at you, so go to the gate, make sure you understand exactly where your plane departs from, then go get your coffee.

23. Always ask for the emergency exit row aisle seat.
If you like being a sardine, don't ask, but any flight attendant or traveler in any country will tell you the normal seats on the plane are uncomfortable and that you are much better off if you get the emergency exit row. I'm shocked at the number of people that file into a plane and sit in their assigned seat without trying to get a better one first.

24. Always ask local residents for their insights.
Get really good at asking questions. You can get so much information if you learn to ask even simple questions. In Patagonia, our guide told us the very best time to come back and hike was December and January. I asked when she herself would come back, and she said between Christmas and New Year's—the weather is great and there aren't many people. It was great advice.

Enjoying an amazing meal in El Calafate, Argentina after getting a tip from a local about the best restaurant in town.

If you don't dig and ask a lot of questions, you're going to miss out on some prime nuggets. On our trip to Chile and Argentina, we always asked our guides what restaurant they would eat at. (I never just ask where a good restaurant is—I want to know the ones the guides go to.) They live there, so they know all the local favorites. They know where the best value and the best quality converge! Some of the best restaurants I've ever eaten at in my life have been on the advice of Santi, our guide in the region. One was a steak house in Bariloche,

Argentina. The other one was in Puerto Varas, Chile, which had the best king crab I've ever eaten in my life. Ask, ask, ask! Dig, dig, dig, and discover gold!

25. *Always double check.*
On a recent trip, we had to turn around no less than five times for people who forgot stuff. Chip and Kathy forgot their coats. Morgan forgot his laptop at one stop and his wallet at another stop...we had to take a ferry back to an island to retrieve it. Lisa forgot her phone at the breakfast table. All this happened in the course of one week! So much time was wasted going back to retrieve these things. Lisa had to do without her iPhone to take pictures in Patagonia for seven days before the phone could finally be transferred to a city and meet up with us. This backtracking could have been avoided with a quick double check each time.

Special delivery...Lisa getting her iPhone back 7 days after she left it at the hotel.

26. *Always say thank you.*
Whatever you do, don't wait until the end of a trip to say thank you. Say it throughout the entire experience, it will change everything. A thank you is the extension of your gratefulness and a grateful heart will make everything infinitely better.

27. *Always pack two days before your trip.*
There are two advantages to doing this. First, it removes all the stress and anxiety of having to pack at the last minute. If you've prepared yourself in advance, you can sit back and enjoy the experience. Second, you give yourself time to mull over the details of the trip and come up with anything you might have not packed. This makes it less likely you're going to forget something, making the trip that much more successful.

28. Always check the five-day weather forecast before you leave.

I use an app called Mega Weather, which gives me a ten-day forecast and a nice overview of what I can expect the weather to be like at my destination. By knowing the weather you are going to encounter on your trip, you can avoid the need to buy clothes you could have brought with you from home. *(Go to the link at the end of this chapter to find out more about the MegaWeather App.)*

This is MegaWeather's ten-day forecast. This is my favorite weather app

29. Always take a look at Google Maps to orient yourself before you arrive.

This helps you create a map in your mind of your destination. You learn where the airport is, where your hotel is, and where the place is you're traveling. It will save you a lot of time because you will be able to understand travel distances, times, and directions better. You'll enjoy your destination so much more if you don't get lost! *(Go to the link at the end of this chapter to find out more about the Google Maps App.)*

GoogleMaps App

30. Always check the local tipping customs in every country you will be visiting.

In many countries, tipping is not necessary, and in other countries, the tip is automatically added to everything you buy. If you do a Google search to learn the norms, you can save yourself a lot of money and angsts.

31. Always check to see if US dollars are widely accepted in a country.

More and more, I find that businesses around the world will accept US dollars, which means you do not have to pay in local currency. When you exchange money, you lose a lot of value through poor exchange rates and high fees, so it is to your advantage to avoid it. Again, it helps to do a quick Google search to find out before you go. For example, if you search "Does Thailand accept US dollars?", You learn that it generally does not. However, if you are in Chile, the last place you would expect them to accept the greenback, many times they do.

32. Always confirm the price and details of any transaction before you commit to it.

When someone quotes you a price, repeat it back to the person and confirm the details. I cannot tell you the number of times I've said yes to something and then I get halfway into the deal and I find out it's costing me much more than I anticipated. Trust me, you can afford taking five seconds to nail down the details.

33. Always confirm and repeat all directions before you leave the person helping you.

Repeating the directions is so important. By doing so, you make sure you didn't misunderstand them and you cement them in your mind.

34. Always take notes immediately on the details.

If someone tells you something, don't tell yourself you will remember it or write it down at a later time. Record everything now, just in time, using one-piece flow and shunning batch work. For example, if someone says let's meet at eight o'clock, immediately set an alarm on your phone for 7:45. It's as simple as saying, "Hey Siri, set an alarm for 7:45." In the time it takes to say those words, your life will become much less complicated, and you will eliminate the ups and downs and unevenness that so many people experience.

Evernote my favorite go-to app for recording all notes and important information

In addition, by writing things down, you force yourself to double check the details of what the person is telling you, confirming there are no defects, no mistakes, and no waste. This saves a lot of grief later. Remember, Lean is all about creating processes that eliminate defects, mistakes, wasted time, and rework. All these tips are clear processes that do exactly that. *(Go to the link at the end of this chapter to find out more about the Evernote App.)*

35. Always compare at least three restaurants before deciding where to eat.

When looking for a restaurant to eat at, I used to always go into the first one that looked good. After dinner, I would continue my stroll down the street, only to find there was a much better restaurant just steps away. Now I make it my practice to review at least three restaurants before I decide where to eat.

36. Always put your razor in a case.

To save weight and space in my suitcase, I switched from an electric razor to a disposable razor. When I packed it for trips, I would toss it into my shaving kit without putting it into a case first. Then one time I reached in to pull the razor out, and those super-sharp four blades slit my finger open like a stuck pig. I spent the next week nursing that very painful cut.

37. Always leave a tip for the maids.

We rarely see them and they work so hard. I always marvel at how clean my room is and how perfectly the bed is made, even when I leave it in such a mess. I love to think about the people we really never see and do something to show them my gratitude.

Always leave a tip for the maid

38. Always build extra margin into everything you do.

If the meeting time is 8:30, don't plan on arriving at 8:30, plan on arriving at least ten minutes early. That way, if something comes up, you will still be early enough to alleviate the stress associated with rushing to get there on time. Being punctual also makes sure you won't be branded inconsiderate by the group you are meeting.

39. Always remember slow is fast.
One time I was rushing to get to my seat on a bus when I moved too quickly up the aisle and caught my coat pocket on one of the seat belt mechanisms, ripping my down coat wide open. Did rushing save me any time? No, it cost me extra time. Worse, I had to find a replacement for my $300 Patagonia coat because I was in a very cold climate—Patagonia, actually—and couldn't afford to go without one. When you start to rush, beware. Slow down—you could save yourself from a costly mistake.

Slow is fast, or the rework will cost you ten times as much time

40. Always keep your roll-on suitcase in the center of the check-in counter and out of sight from the person checking you in.
If you get a check-in agent who is overzealous about the weight limitation, he will make you weigh the suitcase and then make you check it if it is only half a pound over the limit. (It makes no difference whether or not it will fit in the overhead.) If agents can't see your suitcase, they won't question it. Just be prepared when they ask you if you have anything to check—say, "Nope, just carry-on!"

41. Always make a great first impression.
Once when I was on a tour, the tour leader introduced herself, but I was a little distracted and didn't give her the attention I should have. She sized me up immediately as a problem child and everything went downhill from there. Be extra alert when you first meet people (especially leaders) and listen carefully to

their instructions and directions. Put your cell phone away and don't answer e-mails or text messages during this critical first ten-minute introduction. The rest of your trip will go much better.

42. Always pull (not push) your bag down the aisle of an airplane.
There is a powerful concept in the Lean world called "pull and push." You want everyone to pull from you based on their true demand. If you push something on someone there will always be waste. (Think of all the wasted food the airlines pass out that is not eaten, an example of the airlines ignoring lack of demand, *pull*, for the food.) The same goes for how you move down the aisle of an airplane. In this case, remember your Lean principles and pull your suitcase down the aisle. If you want everyone on the aircraft to think you have a low IQ, push your suitcase down the aisle instead of pulling it. You will steer it into the side of the chairs and hold up everyone else on the aircraft. Pulling works much better, in manufacturing and in travel.

44. Always make travel a top priority in your life.
Travel will fill your mind with understanding and your heart with friendships that will transform your life. *(Go to the link at the end of this chapter to get more tips and tricks about planning and traveling your next big adventure.)*

Jimmy Buffet landing on Crooked Island, Bahamas

The One Thing:
A small, consistent routine is 1,000x the power of herculean discipline.

paulakers.net/lt-06

Chapter 7

The Experienced Traveler

It's 5:00 a.m., I'm about ready to board a 30-minute commuter flight from Bellingham to Seattle. I'm sitting close to the gate, answering e-mails as the lines of people crowd together to get on the plane. Instead of joining them, I sit there and remain productive. When the gate agent announces the final boarding, I calmly get up and walk to the counter, having not wasted the ten minutes that everybody else did standing in line. She scans my phone for my boarding pass (no paper, no fumbling to find my ticket) and I head for the plane, where the other passengers are already sitting down.

As I enter the plane, the flight attendant greets me warmly and I return the greeting with a smile. My assigned seat is 2B, a bulkhead seat with better legroom than almost every other seat on the plane. Still, I'm not satisfied. A man is sitting in the seat next to mine, so I quickly scan to see if there is a better one available. To my delight, 1A, an aisle seat at the front of the plane with about six feet of legroom, is open. Without missing a beat, I put my small backpack in the overhead compartment and sit down in the best seat on the plane. The flight attendant briefly explains the emergency exit seat guidelines to me, closes the door, and the engine starts.

Over the course of ten minutes, being an experienced traveler got me:

- Ten precious extra minutes for work.
- A more comfortable seat in the boarding area.
- The best seat on the airplane.
- Onto the plane without having to fight the crowd of people boarding at the same time.

Not a bad way to start the day, but it gets better. We land in Seattle and everyone rushes to grab their bags from the overhead compartments. Again, I do the opposite of the crowd. I sit calmly in my seat and let everyone else exit the plane first. When the plane is completely empty, I look outside and see the others waiting in the cold wind and rain for the bags to be unloaded planeside. They wait for about five minutes, until the cart finally rolls up and everyone squeezes in to grab their bag. The whole time, I remain on the plane, answering e-mails and being productive.

When all the bags except mine are gone, it is time to get off the plane. As I stand up to leave, the flight attendant looks at me and says, "You can always tell an experienced traveler!" I smile warmly at her and thank her for her great service and friendly attitude. On my way out the door, I compliment the pilots for their great landing, walk down the steps, grab my bag, and head for the terminal. Once again, thanks to my experience as a traveler, I gained ten more minutes of productivity and only had to face about thirty seconds of exposure to the wind and rain. My *Lean Travel* principles are really paying off.

I hate waste and I can see it everywhere. I love efficiency and productivity. I love the fact that the vast majority of my life goes smoothly. Every year I receive thousands of e-mails from people all over the world saying how much their life has been transformed as a result of reading my books. They tell me stories of how their work is so much more enjoyable and how their home lives benefit from Lean thinking and continuous improvement. I never tire of hearing these encouraging words—how people improved their lives without any outside help, just because they learned to see waste and see things differently.

A good friend of mine, Loren Jones, says "Once you see waste, you can't un-see it." As soon as you see all the waste that is robbing you of life's joy, you will be compelled to solve your problems and continuously improve everything. Yes, you can transform your life by simply fixing what bothers you. Someone else once sent me an e-mail that illustrates the point with even more clarity: "Lean takes the stupid out of life." Think about it. Every day each of us perform all kinds of processes that have a lot of stupid stuff and struggle in them. *Lean Travel* takes the "stupid" out of travel and replaces it with pure joy and satisfaction.

The satisfaction from today's trip began ahead of schedule. Twenty-four hours before the flight took off, I got a notice from Emirates Airline on my phone that I could check in. I immediately went online and began the check-in process. As I went through the check in, Emirates asked if I would like to upgrade to business class for $1,000. Hell yes I would! The flight was 14 1/2-hours long, and a regular business class ticket cost more than $5,000. Fortunately, I knew from experience and careful observation that the airlines discount these business class seats right before the flight. I also knew that it was important to check in precisely 24 hours before the flight to get the best chance of purchasing one of these discounted seats.

A thousand dollars was a small price to pay for such a big improvement. Being in business class allows me to continually work the entire flight, which is invaluable to me because my time is so valuable. My time is valuable because I'm very productive, which makes people willing to pay me more than most people would ever dream of. Thus, my Lean thinking not only makes me more productive, it makes me more valuable and allows me to experience some of the finer things in life. You can see why I say, "I don't like Lean. I love Lean!"

When I get off the commuter flight, I have not yet received an electronic or paper boarding pass for my next flight, so I go to the Emirates Airline gate where the plane will be leaving in approximately two hours. There's no one there except one gate agent. I pick up my boarding pass (avoiding going outside security to the normal check-in area) and ask the agent what time I should be back at the gate. He tells me the plane will board at 8:00 and will be in the air at 9:00, with the doors closing at 8:40. I double check to make sure that if I arrive at 8:30 I'll be sufficiently on time. He says absolutely, so I pull out my iPhone and tell Siri to set an alarm for 8:15. Siri replies that my alarm is set.

With extra time on my hands, I walk to the Alaska Airlines Board Room (Alaska's lounge) to work quietly and eat breakfast. At the front desk, I hand the receptionist my lounge club card, tell her I do not need a receipt (which would only add waste to the process), and head inside.

For breakfast, I would like a latte, an apple, and two hard-boiled eggs. If it were your first time visiting the Board Room, you might struggle to find these items, because the automatic espresso and latte machine is downstairs and the apples and hard-boiled eggs are upstairs. This is where your *Lean Travel* skills will help you out. As I mentioned in Chapter 5, when you go somewhere new, it's best to get the lay of the land before you commit to a restaurant. This is true wherever you are, including airport lounges, so when you visit a lounge for the first time, walk through the entire place to understand what is available. If there is more than one level, explore them all. If you don't, you might miss something important. I can't tell you the number of times in the Board Room that people have asked me where I got an apple, and when I told them upstairs, they said they didn't even know there was an upstairs.

I grab my free latte and walk toward the elevator, but the line is very long. Waiting is a waste and I will have no part of it, so I swing my backpack onto my back, pick up my suitcase, and walk up the stairs. The beauty of this is I am getting more exercise and not sitting there unproductively waiting for an elevator to haul a fat, sloppy body to the second floor. I have turned the management of my health into a process, and am always looking for every opportunity to exercise and eat correctly, even opportunities as small as a one-flight walk up the stairs.

Always take the stairs.

Every second is precious and I try to always deliver value and improve the quality of my life. If you think I'm obsessive about improvement, consider this: Everywhere I go, people tell me they want my life! I tell them they can have it if they learn to see waste and think Lean!

When my friends ask, "Paul, how do you do it?" The answer is really quite simple: I just learn from my experiences. There's nothing magical about me or my knowledge. Once you figure out how to deliberately learn from your experiences, you no longer allow stupidity to become a common habit that hurts your success. In order to learn effectively, you have to understand a few tools, and the most important one of all is learning to see waste. This is the key to becoming a successful experienced traveler. *(Go to the link at the end of this chapter to explore the board room.)*

> **The One Thing:**
> *Open your eyes-waste is everywhere. Your wealth and the quality life you seek will be found by eliminating your waste.*

paulakers.net/lt-07

Chapter 8

All We Need is Fat Navy SEALs

The goal of this book is to help people live better lives by traveling smarter, and teach them to learn and improve by incorporating the best practices they observe in the different cultures they experience. It has always been my goal to be positive and not seek to point out the negative or be negative. That said, this chapter is a blunt call to action for my fellow Americans. It contains a harsh message, because I love my people and my country so much that I am compelled to share it. If you're not an American, don't point fingers at us—we all have problems.

Elite troops in the US military

Whenever I think about the Navy SEALs, the most elite troops in the entire US military, I think of people who are the epitome of physical conditioning and mental toughness. I say this with first-hand knowledge because I have a few friends who are Navy SEALs. No matter where they are in the world, enemies of the United States tremble at the thought of being hunted down by one of these highly-trained warriors.

The SEALs are held to extremely demanding standards of physical fitness, which sets them far apart from the physical condition of most Americans. If the average American were sent out to pursue our enemies, they would be laughed at and return without succeeding. Why? Because we are the fattest, sloppiest people on earth. I warned you the message was harsh.

Demanding standards for physical fitness

It doesn't matter where I go in the US, almost everyone seems to be obese. This is not the case in other countries. I've traveled to over sixty countries, and it's rare to find one where the majority of the population is fat and overweight. I just returned from a month in South America, where I marveled at how many people were reasonably sized. Coming back to the United States,

I was hit upside the head by the disgusting and sloppy nature of most Americans. It seemed as though we've accepted that the official symbol of being an American is to be 50-80 pounds overweight.

Not too long ago, I brought a delegation of high-level international business leaders to the US on a tour of different companies. Near the end of the trip, one of the American managers we met graciously offered each of my guests a golf pullover from his company. It was a wonderful gesture, but there was one problem: they were too big. The average weight of the people from my delegation was 150 pounds, and the box of golf shirts was sized for people like the Americans around us, most weighing 280-350 pounds each. When our host opened the box to let them choose the size, right on the top were several 3XL-sized pullovers. (When I saw that, I knew we were in trouble.) We went through the whole box and found only three mediums; the rest were too large. Our host sheepishly apologized, commenting that the pullovers were sized for "big Americans." I thought to myself, you mean fat Americans!

Don't get me wrong, I love America and think it's the greatest country on earth, but I was very embarrassed. We should all be ashamed of our ridiculous gluttony. My international guests were thinking the same thing. You could see it in their eyes.

Our weight problem is everywhere. As I went through security at the airport this morning, I thought to myself it must be required to be obese in order to work for the TSA. As that thought passed through my mind, a policeman walked by who looked like he was nine months pregnant. (Does anyone in America respect their body?) Everyone is fat, and not just a little fat! We have conditioned ourselves to think this is normal, when in reality, it is disgusting!

I know you think I am

Obesity has taken over the US.

exaggerating, but look around. I challenge you to find people who are trim and fit in America; they are few and far between. The average American looks three to nine months pregnant, including men! Just now, as I was boarding my plane from Denver

Bad food is EVERYWHERE!

to Seattle, there was a guy so big that he was hanging six inches over both sides of his seat and into the aisle. I could not get my rolling suitcase by him, so he had to lean over and envelope the guy next to him just so I could get past.

What causes this type of obesity? I'll bet anyone a thousand bucks that if you're fat and overweight, it's not because of your genes. It's more likely because you eat shitty food. Look around at all the people who are overweight and then watch what they eat. Add it up, the math is simple! We need about 2,400 to 3,000 calories a day, not 5,000 to 7,000!

If you're going to stop me and tell me about the corporate conspiracy to make us fat, or that our schools are not educating our kids about proper nutrition, or that the government is disseminating misinformation, I don't want to hear any of it. This is simply about personal responsibility and people engaging their brains. Good information and bad information are everywhere, and we need to

Before...and...After.

use our brains to figure out which is which. Our brains are our most powerful asset and we have completely left them on the sidelines when it comes to nutrition and food. Personal responsibility does wonders and if each person had more of it, we could solve 99.9% of our problems. We cannot go around blaming someone else for them. *(Go to the link at the end of this chapter to learn more about eating healthy.)*

I speak from experience, and can very easily point the

finger at myself. I spent most of the last thirty years of my adult life overweight and unhealthy. I didn't understand the amazing gift my body was and abused it regularly. Consuming poor-quality, sugary food and having a lackluster exercise routine was all it took to make me look like everyone else in America. Then I woke up from my stupor and recaptured the health I always dreamed about. My transformation was so compelling that I wrote a book about my journey called Lean Health. It was not a hard transformation; it was an intelligent transformation that didn't require mountains of willpower. It simply required the intelligence of a fifth grader and the honesty of a kindergartner.

Today, I walk through airports and convenience stores all the time and am never tempted to eat all the junk food that's available. The corporate marketing ploys are still in place trying to lure us to eat things that are deleterious to our health, but they don't matter because:

I now understand.
I changed my mind.
I educated myself.
I used the potential of my brain.
I stopped making stupid excuses.
I stopped being a dumbass.
I stopped blaming other people.
I took responsibility.
I started documenting the facts.
I started understanding the facts.
I started running experiments.
I started analyzing information
I started thinking critically.
I took action.

During my entire transformation, I never blamed anyone but

myself. It was my stupidity that put my health in a compromising position and it was my intelligence and common sense that lifted me out of it. If I blamed my problems on someone else, I wouldn't have done any of those things and I wouldn't have gained any of those tools or resources for personal development. Blaming poor health on anyone or anything else is a crock of shit. We have a free will—there are no handcuffs on any of us! *(Go to the link at the end of this chapter to find out more about the Paul's Ironman Challenge.)*

One the things I really enjoy about travel, apart from dodging all the garbage in the airports and convenience stores, is the voluminous amounts of fresh fruits and vegetables I find all over the world. People in other countries are not exposed to the same amount of prepackaged crap we Americans eat. Food is for nourishment. It is not to mask pain and fill voids in our unbalanced psychologies.

Voluminous amounts of fresh foods.

    Here's my advice: Stop opening packages when you eat. Instead, peel a banana, bite into an apple, taste and enjoy fruits and vegetables. You won't believe what you've been missing. Eat plants, not things made in a plant! I'm not a vegetarian, but I have changed my diet to make sure 80% of it comes from fruits and vegetables. I get my protein from fish, chicken and nuts. Everything is so simple.

Instead of lowering our standards for what it means to be healthy, we need to raise our standards. We would never dumb down the requirements for our elite Navy SEALs. Can you imagine: "Hey, First Lieutenant Stevenson, your mission is to go capture and kill the bad guys in Afghanistan, and by the way, don't worry about your beer belly, I am sure you won't have to chase them down." We shouldn't dumb them down for ourselves. Our children, law enforcement, business and political leaders, teachers, professors, bus drivers, health professionals, doctors, scientists, pilots, mothers, and fathers are fat and grossly overweight. For the love of God America, wake up! Not even the Navy SEALs can protect you from this stupidity! *(Go to the link at the end of this chapter to find out all the weird fruit Paul has tried on all his travels.)*

> **The One Thing:**
> America, open your eyes! The world is shaking its head at you.

paulakers.net/lt-08

Chapter 9

Horse's Ass or Diplomat

Patagonia

I am a AAA personality (triple Type A). I am not passive. I am very determined. When I have a goal, I go after it and I will not quit until I achieve it. In the past, I was perfectly capable of tearing someone a new one if they crossed me the wrong way. However, I've learned through the process of continuous improvement how to temper myself in the most trying situations.

It is important that as humans we are continually reflective. The Japanese word for this is hansei, which means to reflect on actions and improve them over and over again. With my strong leadership tendencies, it was important to embrace this philosophy, lest I become bound to always getting my way and hence never learn or improve.

Paul and Leanne in a beautiful 200 year old wooden church on Chiloe' Island

What follows is an epic story of self-control and continuous improvement. In it, I achieved an extremely favorable outcome in the most unfavorable circumstances, largely because of my determination to reinvent myself and not settle for business as usual. In the past, I typically didn't concern myself with other people's approval, but this time, I could see clearly that if I ignored public opinion, it wouldn't matter how right I was, I would lose this epic battle. In my wildest imagination I could not have written a story with more twists, turns, and drama.

The plot unfolded around a month-long trip my wife Leanne and I took to Chile, Argentina, Easter Island, Brazil, and Patagonia. It was a trip we had been looking forward to for a long time. Both of us are busy executive leaders in our company, FastCap. She gets to work at 6 a.m. every day, and if she's lucky she leaves at 7 p.m. For nine months of the year, I travel, speak, and consult all over the globe, so whenever we get time to be together, it is a special and important time.

For this trip, Leanne did most of the planning. She organized the trip through a tour company called Overseas Adventure Travel

Having dinner at a home in Buenos Aires.

(OAT). It was our second major trip with OAT. In 2015, we took a fantastic one-month trip with OAT to Southeast Asia. We were so happy with our experience that we had already booked an additional one-month trip to Australia and New Zealand in 2017 and were in the planning stages of an additional trip to Antarctica during the same time period. We are still friends with the group leaders and the new friends we made on that trip.

In Southeast Asia, I produced thirteen videos documenting the trip, which had thousands of views and preserved many wonderful memories for our entire group. They also proved to be great marketing tools for OAT. After seeing them, our good friend Dana wanted to join us on the trip to South America, as did a new couple, Morgan and Lisa Lohman, who had never traveled outside the United States before. They saw the videos and wanted in on the adventure. Everyone was expecting to have a great trip.

Prior to our departure, Leanne corresponded several times with our group leader, Graciela, to make sure we had everything we needed for the adventure. Their communication was cordial and non-eventful, but the calm was misleading. Yvon Chouinard, the founder of Patagonia, said that "real adventure starts when everything goes wrong." Not only was everything about to go wrong, but the shit was going to hit the fan and I would be tested for intelligence and political sagacity.

On the first leg of the trip, Leanne and I flew into Santiago, Chile, where we met up with the rest of our group. We really did not know what to expect, though we had traveled extensively throughout Mexico, Central America, Cuba, and the Caribbean, and we loved the Spanish and Latin cultures. South America was a continent we definitely wanted to discover, with its rich diversity of cultures and European influence. One thing for sure: our expectations were high and we were looking forward to seeing new places, especially the enchanting region of Patagonia.

At the airport in Santiago, we were met by our local guide, Paul. Paul was warm, friendly, and outgoing—everything we had come to experience with the other guides we had in Southeast Asia—but we both thought it was odd that Graciela did not meet us herself. Normally, the primary trip leader would meet us at the airport because she would be in charge throughout the duration of the trip. It was not a big deal, but it was a little strange.

When we first met Graciela at the hotel, she didn't seem as warm as we expected. She asked us how our flight was and my wife exclaimed, "It was awesome." Graciela looked at her with no expression and uttered "Oh," as if to say, "Aren't you a strange bird? Who says 'awesome' after spending sixteen hours on a plane?" My first thought was maybe she was not a happy person, but I quickly put this aside and allowed her to continue her lackluster orientation. For whatever reason, Graciela just didn't seem excited about the huge adventure we were all about to embark on. Unfortunately, her attitude went downhill from there.

We got our room keys and went upstairs. To our surprise, the room had three single beds in a very small and crowded space. Unhappy with the three-star accommodations, I picked up the phone and asked the desk manager if they had a room with one queen bed instead. He said no, and this was all they could give us. Again, we were surprised at how the trip was starting. OAT is not a cheap outfit, and it usually provided at least four-star accommodations, unless we were staying in a very remote location. Santiago, Chile, is not remote at all.

I knew Graciela was still down in the lobby, so I asked the desk manager if he would put her on the phone. I explained my concern to her and she snapped at me and told me that having single beds was the standard! I was shocked. I was the customer and she was telling me I was wrong and didn't want to help! I explained that we never had this kind of accommodations on our previous trip with OAT, and she again barked at me that I was wrong. I told her I didn't think she was listening to me and that I hadn't come on a month-long vacation with my wife to sleep in separate beds.

She retorted that I wasn't listening to her. At that moment, I knew I was going to lose the battle and that I needed to back off and get away from a very tense situation. I pulled the phone away from my ear and lowered it very slowly to the cradle without saying a word. Graciela's hostility was palpable, and I felt I needed to back away or something bad was going to happen. A few minutes later, the phone rang and she asked me to come down to have a meeting with her in fifteen minutes. No problem, I told her. I would be on time.

Before I made it downstairs, my wife went to the lobby. Graciela came up to her and told her she would not be disrespected. Leanne explained we weren't disrespecting her, we simply requested a bed together. Graciela told her the queen and king beds were for the single customers and couples were only given a bed together if they requested it beforehand. Leanne replied that when we traveled with OAT before we never had do that. Graciela stuck to her guns and said that was not how it worked.

When I arrived soon thereafter, Graciela held out her hand and said, "Hello, I'm Graciela. Let's start over." Her tone was gruff and authoritative, but I held out my hand and shook hers and said okay. She explained to me that if we were going to be together I needed to give her respect. I said in a very quiet, respectful voice, "Respect is something that's earned."

Apparently, that wasn't what Graciela wanted to hear. She began to insult me again and called me a "machine" in a very demeaning fashion. It was an odd comment, but I guess she said it because I was so measured and showed no emotion. I knew being emotional would do nothing but exacerbate the situation. Graciela was charged and looking for a fight and I was running as fast as I could. Believe me, avoiding confrontation is not in my nature. My willingness to not fight with her came from the continuous improvement I've implemented in order to make myself more agreeable in a group setting. I am a strong leader and am fully aware that sometimes you have to be willing to follow and not always lead. The conversation with Graciela was going to go nowhere, so I quietly walked away. We did not speak much to each other the rest of the day.

The next morning, Graciela confronted me again at breakfast. I was minding my own business, eating and talking with my friends and my wife when she cornered me, demanding my respect. Up to this point, I had attended every meeting and outing into the city, always being attentive and never doing anything to distract from the group. I minded my own business and tried to steer clear of Graciela's hostile demeanor.

Nonetheless, she was relentless and I again walked away without saying a word. There was no way you could have a conversation with her. She was hostile from start to finish. Her agenda was clear. She wanted me to grovel and say I was wrong, when all I had done was ask for a queen bed. In my mind, this was a very minimal standard for a trip that costs thousands of dollars. The last thing that would be appropriate in this situation would be to apologize for expecting something so basic.

The next day she confronted me again and demanded I leave the trip right before we were ready to leave for Easter Island. I told her I was not prepared to do that. She got in my face, but I did not respond to her. I was not about to allow this woman to destroy a very special vacation that my wife and I had been looking forward to for over a year.

We all boarded the bus and headed to the airport. When we arrived to check in, Graciela did not have a ticket for me. She had already canceled it, thinking I would back out. When she saw that I did not, she had to scramble to secure a ticket for me so I could get on the plane with the rest of the group. Despite her antics, I never said a word to her or showed any disapproval in any way at all.

When we got to Easter Island, we had about three hours before our next scheduled event, so Morgan and I decided to rent a scooter and a four-wheeler to

Morgan and I goofing off on Easter Island

go exploring. When it was time for the bus to leave, we asked Graciela if we could follow the bus to our next outing, and she seemed to have no objection. When it was time to go, we pulled in behind the bus on our scooter and four-wheeler and prepared to follow it. To our astonishment, the bus pulled out and sped away from us at over sixty miles an hour (on a dirt road!). We took off in hot pursuit, like policemen on a high-speed chase.

Morgan has no inhibition. He has his cell phone tucked into his underwear while shopping at a local craft shop on Easter Island ....Morgan took the Lean thing very seriously.

At first, we managed to keep up, although barely. I ride motorcycles at a very high level and it was everything I could do to keep up with the bus, which was going around corners at speeds that seemed totally unsafe. Eventually, though, we had to give up. Morgan fell behind first—his scooter was too slow. My quad was faster, but even when maxed out it couldn't stay with the bus, which was flying. We admitted our defeat and slowed down. When we got to the town we were scheduled to visit, Morgan and I crisscrossed up and down the roads looking for the group, but to no avail. We never found it.

Morgan and I ran out of clothes, so we thought we would go super Lean and resorted to our underwear...surprisingly comfortable, fast drying, and they double as a bathing suit. We only got a few strange looks.

Later on in the afternoon, we reconnected with everyone back at our hotel. I asked my wife what happened and she said the group couldn't figure out what was going on. The bus was driving so fast that the women were squealing as it went around corners. The only thing I could figure is that Graciela told the bus driver to lose us, so he drove at ridiculous speeds to do it. The irony of the story is that she had told us we were visiting a quiet little island where everyone moved at a very slow speed and that we needed to tone down all of our expectations because things happen very slowly.

The trip only got stranger from there. The next thing you know, Graciela was barking at Leanne for being a few minutes late to the bus (along with two other people). Graciela waved her finger in my wife's face and said if she was ever late again they would leave without her. Leanne apologized over and over, but Graciela wouldn't stop. She continued to reprimand her in front of everyone until she started crying. Other passengers tried to console Leanne by saying they thought Graciela was out of line and they were sorry she was being so mean. It was clear that Graciela was taking out her disapproval of me on my wife. Other people were often late and were never scolded. In fact, Graciela herself was late and held the rest of the group up and no one paid any attention to it—that's just part of traveling with a group. My wife's tardiness was inconsequential compared to other people's, yet she received a scolding that was completely uncalled for. We were beginning to wonder whether this trip was a good idea or not.

Running in front of Muhi on Easter Island was an epic experience.

Surprisingly, the rest of the three days on Easter Island were relatively uneventful. I was able to steer clear of Graciela and not have any incidents. We had a fantastic time, but she was clearly not the friendly leader we had expected. She had very little energy and was not excited about anything, unlike the rest of us. The experience that we had on Easter Island was epic, and I was having a great time documenting the entire trip. I was committed to having

Beautiful view of the highest building of South America.

the trip of a lifetime and that's exactly what I was doing, with the exception of dealing with Graciela with her abrupt and unfriendly disposition.

We flew back to Santiago to stay one night before we went to Buenos Aires to meet up with the rest of the main trip travelers. While we were away, OAT had evidently decided that the first hotel was substandard and had changed to a new one. It was just blocks from the previous hotel and much better. We all commented that if we had just stayed at this new hotel in the first place, there would not have been any problems at all.

The next morning, our group flew to Buenos Aries for a few days before going on to our next location, the region of Patagonia. In Buenos Aires, we went to a tango bar and had a fantastic meal while enjoying a great dance show. During the entire time, Graciela stayed away from the group. My wife thought she saw Graciela in the very

Sampling fantastic South American wine and food

back of the room making phone calls during the show, but thought nothing of it. Afterward, we all got back on the bus and she asked us how we liked it. We all said it was wonderful. Then Graciela made a very odd comment. She said, with great gusto, "I am so happy!" We thought it was strange because up to that moment, she was not happy about anything.

We got back to the hotel room around midnight, and Leanne went to check in for the flight the next morning to Bariloche. She became alarmed when she noticed the flight that was supposed to take us to Seattle three weeks later had been rescheduled, and we were now booked to fly home to United States the next morning! We couldn't believe it! Leanne spent the next four hours on the phone and working with the airlines to see what had transpired. I also sent e-mails to OAT in United States saying we had a very serious problem and we needed their assistance. We received no response.

When we called the airline, they told us they changed our ticket because we had called and changed it. My wife informed them we did not call and change anything. This seemed strange. We called OAT again and they replied that

Leanne and I were left high and dry in an unfamiliar city where we didn't speak the language

yes, they had spoken to Leanne earlier in the day and she had changed the ticket. My wife told the agent that she had never talked to OAT or the airline. At that point, the agent on the line began to put everything together and realized that Graciela had called and impersonated my wife, using our passport numbers to change all the airline tickets. All of a sudden, the OAT agent on the phone was doing some serious backpedaling. She promised they would call us back, but never did. OAT wasn't taking responsibility for anything. The agent knew Graciela had committed fraud by impersonating Leanne. The one upside was we now had some clue about what Graciela was up to, so the next morning, rather than being completely caught off guard, we were prepared for something crazy to happen. Needless to say, we only slept about an hour that night. By the time we sorted through everything that transpired, it was five in the morning and we had to wake up at six to leave.

As we got ready to leave the hotel for the airport, Graciela walked up to me with a large envelope and said, "Paul you're no longer on the trip. You and your wife are going home." She handed me what appeared to be airline tickets in a large white envelope. I quietly told her I was not going anywhere, that this was my vacation, and that I was staying on the trip. I refused the tickets and walked away. Graciela insisted and said we were no longer on the trip. I began to walk toward the bus as all the other people on the tour looked on in total shock. Two people from OAT's office in Buenos Aires were there to support Graciela in her devious plan. Now we knew why Graciela was so happy the night before; she had spent the evening lying, distorting and conniving with the OAT management to throw us off the trip.

I couldn't believe it—this all happened because we wanted a queen bed together! I went to the bus and tried to get on, but two or three men and a woman from the Argentina office blocked our path. I was quiet and did not push. I did nothing but stand there trying to get on the bus as they let everyone besides Leanne and me get on the bus. The whole situation was surreal. It was hard to believe what was happening. It was the craziest thing I've ever heard of.

Desperately trying to get our tickets reissued, after Graciela cancelled them three times.

As the other passengers boarded the bus, they told the OAT managers they were making a huge mistake and that they didn't have the facts and didn't know what had been going on. When the bus was loaded, the door shut and my wife and I were left standing on the streets of Buenos Aires, watching the bus drive away without us. Leanne was in tears. When I looked at her, I thought, oh my gosh, this cannot be happening. I can't let this happen to her.

About 60 seconds later, we came to our senses and quickly hailed a cab. As we drove away, the OAT employee chased our cab and yelled, asking where we were going. We told her she kicked us off the trip, so what business of hers was it? We decided to at

Exploring a beautiful gaucho shop in Buenos Aires.

least go to the airport and try to get on the flight to Bariloche. We thought we could salvage the trip by renting a car in Patagonia. We knew the agenda so we could at least go and visit the same places, even if we were not with the group. Leanne had been able to get us checked in the night before on the flight from Buenos Aires to Bariloche. OAT had cancelled our main flight home, but hadn't touched our in-country flights, so we thought we would be able to get on the plane.

    We got into the same line as our tour group, but when Graciela saw us, she went up to the counter and spoke to the agent. When we got up to the desk to check our bags, the agents said we had been removed from the flight and had no tickets for us. We both showed them our phones that had our check-in information and boarding passes, but they said we were not in the system. Somehow, Graciela was able to get our ticket cancelled. How she had the power to get the airline to do this was staggering. She spoke in Spanish, so we don't know what she said. The whole group was watching all this take place and confused at how she could treat a customer this way. When we realized everyone was in cahoots with Graciela, we quickly grabbed our bags and went to another counter, where Leanne was able to find someone to help her.

    At the next counter, the LAN Airline agent was mystified at how we could have been removed from our flight. Thankfully, he was not a part a Graciela's maniacal scheme, so he simply re-issued the ticket and put us back on the flight. While Leanne was working with the new ticket agent, I was on the phone with one of OAT's top agents, Elizabeth, pleading with her to help us. She would have none of it. She completely agreed with Graciela and was not interested in hearing my side of the story. She said the decision had been made and we were removed from the trip. I explained that they didn't even do their due diligence. They didn't ask anybody else on the trip, nor did they call guides that we had worked with in Southeast Asia. I asked them to ask somebody for the facts, but she refused. I repeated over and over, in a very calm tone, that OAT was making a massive mistake, but she insisted we were off the trip.

Regardless, we proceeded to the gate with our newly issued tickets and we took our place in line. Graciela saw us coming and went over to the gate agents, speaking in Spanish to them for a while. When the agents scanned our tickets, they pulled us aside and said there was a problem with them. We asked what was wrong, but they ignored us. We asked for a manager and they ignored us again. Soon, everyone had boarded and we were left standing there speechless. Three times, right in front of us, Graciela was able to get LAN airlines to cancel tickets we had been issued. After the plane had been loaded for ten minutes, the airline employees were still trying to figure out what to do with the two of us. I had never seen anything like it.

A picture of Santi and his good friends serving us an authentic Argentinian dinner at a gaucho ranch in Patagonia.

Finally, for reasons that are still unclear, the agents came to their senses and said the tickets were valid. They scanned us through and we walked onto the plane, shocked and relieved at the same time. We could not believe the drama that had just unfolded over the last two hours. We were kicked off the trip, had to get a cab without speaking the language, and figure out what airport to go to. Then we were kicked off our flight three times, but were able to negotiate to get new tickets in a domestic airport that we had never been to before. Now we were back on track, walking up the aisle of the flight to Bariloche. Graciela had the most disgusted look on her face as we walked by, but we didn't acknowledge her. We minded our own business and sat down.

Making my impromptu videos with all the wonderful people I meet.

When we landed in Bariloche, we went to get our checked bags. Graciela stood across the baggage carousel from

Visiting a small community school and letting the children interact with my drone.

us, fully engrossed in a telephone conversation, with a very upset look on her face. We grabbed our bags and went to rent a car and find somewhere to stay. Our fellow travelers looked at us in dismay. One woman was crying and many of them said good luck and we are so sad this is happening to you. Graciela had really put everyone in a difficult place. Our friends traveling with us were upset, but they were also worried she would retaliate against them and get them kicked off the trip. Our new friends were clearly not happy with what had transpired, but they were afraid to go against her as well.

    We ended up deciding to stay at a different hotel than the rest of the group, thinking it best not to rub it in that we made it to Bariloche despite Graciela's plan. We were trying to make the best of a bad situation, even though it was at a great expense to us—over $800 for the hotel and car alone, not to mention the costs to come as we traveled onward. OAT had ended the conversation with me saying they were standing by the decision to cancel all our flights and we were on our own to make our way through South America. When we scheduled the trip we had told OAT we were planning to go to Iguazu Falls by ourselves after the official trip ended. We had already booked those flights and hotels on our own, so we planned to stay and meet back up with our friends when the tour was over in about three weeks. We spent the day making our way to our hotel and getting situated. We let our friends know where we were staying and made the best we could of a strange situation.

    Later when we were at dinner, I received a call from Elizabeth at OAT. She told us they had replaced Graciela with a new trip leader and we were welcome to join up with the group in the morning. We said we would. We didn't ask how or why that decision was made. We took the high road and decided to just move on and join the group. The new leader, Santiago, e-mailed us to meet him at the group hotel in the morning. When we met him, we were very pleased he didn't seem to harbor any preconceived ideas that we were "problem" people. We made it a point not to talk about what had happened with everyone, but instead, to forget what happened and move on.

I meet amazing people everywhere I go. ***Left Image:*** *This man stayed up late at night to custom make a scarf and hat for me, so when I left the next morning it would be ready.* ***Middle Image:*** *Martin, the owner of a cheese and wine store, let us sample his wonderful cheeses and meats.* ***Right Image:*** *Gloria gave us exceptional service at this gaucho shop in Buenos Aires.*

The rest of the trip was amazing. Santiago and the local guides at each place were so good. Other travelers thought it was a blessing in disguise that we had to experience what we did so the group could have a better trip leader. Santi was friendly, happy, informative, and fun. We ended up with a great outcome, in spite of the bad attitude and continued efforts of Graciela to derail our trip. Thankfully, I had made improvements in the way I deal with difficult situations before we went on this trip.

One thing is for sure: you should not expect all your travels to go perfectly. There will always be problems and ups and downs, but if you embrace Lean thinking and continuous improvement in the way you pack, plan, and improve your disposition and attitude, your travels will generate fantastic stories that you will tell over a glass of wine for years to come.

Speaking of stories, did I tell you the one about binoculars in Africa? Keep reading… *(Go to the link at the end of this chapter to see Paul run around the world!)*

The One Thing:
Stay calm and your travels will become stories to tell over a fine glass of wine.

---

paulakers.net/lt-09

Chapter 10

Know the Facts, Understand the Details

Africa is a land that seems so far away for most of us. For a long time, I dreamed of going to Africa and going on safari, but it appeared out of reach. Could I afford to go there? Would I ever be able to make the time to go to a land so far away? With its multiple languages and cultures, how could I negotiate the unfamiliar environment successfully? I had lots of questions and certainly not all the answers, but I kept trying to find them.

In the Lean world, we emphasize the necessity to observe, ask questions, and fully understand the facts before we proceed to make changes or improvements. This deliberate approach makes problem solving more effective. When I teach Lean, I sometimes give this example: If you're a marksman and you're into handling guns properly, you might have heard the saying that "slow is smooth, smooth is fast." If you jerk the gun, if you try to pull it out too quickly, you're more than likely going to miss. But if you're smooth and slow, you're more likely to hit the target every time and thus achieve your objective. The same goes for Lean problem solving. Take the time to get the facts and know the facts so you will not have any unwanted surprises.

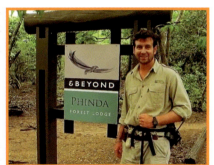

James, our guide at Phinda Forest &Beyond is the top notch organization we chose for our first trip to Africa.

When I was fifty-two years old, I finally had the opportunity to visit Africa, one of my major dreams in life. My wife and I were very thorough with the trip planning. We wanted to get things right. We spent much of a year trying to figure out who we would work with in order to explore the continent. We finally settled on &Beyond, a top-tier African tour company based in South Africa. We took along our good friends Cindy and Gordon, who were a total hoot and fun to be with. Just like most of our trips, there would be a few twists and turns, and Cindy and Gordon would be in on all of them with us. The four of us were ready to have a fantastic time.

The trip would be full of firsts for me: my first time on

an Airbus 380 (an amazing double-decker airplane), my first time seeing lions in the wild, my first time walking with a cheetah in the bush, and my first time seeing a leopard in a tree just after it had made a kill. I could never put into words everything we saw, but I made a video for each day I was in Africa, so it is all documented.

We met up with our friends at JFK airport in New York, where we boarded the A380. Upon arriving in Johannesburg, South Africa, our guide picked us up at the airport and drove us two hours to our first camp, the Phinda Forest Lodge, where we would begin our safari. The whole idea of a safari is to take you to the middle of nowhere, but I guess I didn't realize just what that meant—I mean, we were in the middle of nowhere! As we approached the camp we had to drive through a small African village where people were selling things on the dirt streets. Everything seemed very primitive, and I was nervous that our lodging would be primitive too. We paid a lot of money to go on this trip and I was expecting some nice accommodations. We had worked very hard to do our research and we didn't want any surprises. As we approached the entrance to the camp, we only saw one small wooden bench sitting beside the road. The driver stopped, got out, and said, "Okay, you're home!"

I thought to Cindy and Gordon were going to kill me because I had just made them spend over $20,000 and it looked like we were about to get ripped off. My lips were trembling, but I got out of the car without protesting. Before long, a young man showed up with a wheelbarrow, loaded it with our luggage, and began to roll it up a narrow dirt trail and through the bushes. I followed along, wondering what was going on. Were they going to walk us into the bushes and mug us, take our money and passports and leave us for the wild animals? I had anticipated driving up to a grand entrance with a

Arriving at Phinda Forest to a bench, a sign, and a dirt path. "Did we just get ripped off?"

large porte cochère, where a bellman would greet us with a nice hot latte, not walking up a narrow dirt path through the brush.

My fears were premature though. After about five minutes, the path opened up into a beautiful clearing where there was a fantastic lodge overlooking the savanna, with wild animals everywhere. The porter showed us to the room where we would stay. As we walked down the trail, a man carrying a spear went with us, just in case an unfriendly animal jumped out of the bushes. Our private tent was nothing short of five stars and stunningly beautiful. Best of all, it was in the middle of nowhere. You could not see anyone as soon as the porter and guard left. All you could hear was the commotion from the wild animals around us.

Our fantastic tent, nestled in the woods, surrounded by nature and wild animals, exceeding our wildest imaginations.

The porter cautioned that when we wanted to leave the cabin we needed to call and have the guard come and escort us to the lodge. Walking around by yourself was not an option here. We were also warned never to leave the door open. In fact, once we opened the door for a bit too long and a monkey ran in and stole an apple from our fruit basket. We would not be disappointed at all by the &Beyond experience. It was nothing short of over the top! *(Go to the link at the end of this chapter to find out more about &Beyond.)*

Later that afternoon, after we settled into our rooms, we went on our first game drive. We loaded into an open vehicle with James, our ranger. Everyone was so excited—we were on safari in Africa! For the next couple hours, we drove around, frequently stopping for James to point out interesting animals, plants, and other unique features of the landscape. Many were right next to the Land Cruiser, but some were very small or way off in the distance, so James used a pair of binoculars to identify them.

Neither Gordon, Cindy, Leanne, or I had thought to bring binoculars, and after an hour of passing the binoculars around between us, we decided we needed to get some for ourselves.

When we got back to camp we went to the tiny gift store at the lodge. Inside the store, a small, locked glass case contained two pairs of binoculars, exactly what we needed. I asked the sales assistant if we could try them out, and she nodded. She opened the cabinet and handed me the binoculars. I took them outside to observe a bird that was about twenty feet away. "Oh my gosh!" I exclaimed. I had never looked through a pair of binoculars that clear and sharp before.

The young woman did not speak much English, but I was able to inquire how much they were. Using a calculator, we figured they cost $350, based on the current exchange rate. The price seemed a bit expensive, but we were in the middle of nowhere and they were excellent quality. I wasn't planning on coming back to Africa anytime soon, and I really wanted to be able to see everything without having to wait for the others to finish using the binoculars. What the heck, I thought. It sounds like a reasonable proposition.

I was about to buy them when the clerk told me something that was a little curious. She said I could rent the binoculars if I wanted to. I calculated the cost of renting them versus buying them and there wasn't much difference, so I decided to buy them. (Man, did I have the facts screwed up on this one!). I was in a bit of a hurry because we were only about ten minutes away from another game drive and I wanted to secure the binoculars and get on the truck to start looking at all the cool things James had been pointing out.

At this point, I should have reminded myself to slow down. Get the facts, know the facts, understand the facts, and you won't have any unwanted surprises. There were so many warning signs, but I ignored them.

Now, after having traveled to

Our $3,000+ binoculars that we thought were $300.

over 60 countries, I am keenly aware of those cues and they will never go unnoticed. I travel with other people and I see them miss things all the time and they end up with the unwanted surprises—the cab fare that costs three times more than they thought, the tour that didn't include five additional things, the dinner that was twice as expensive as first thought, etc.—all because they ignored the facts and didn't take the time to make sure there was clarity with the information that was being given them.

A few minutes later Cindy came by and I told her about the great binoculars I had just found that were not really that expensive. She quickly ran into the gift store and asked to look at the other pair in the case. She tried them and was amazed at how good they were. She was also happy because they were only $300 and she felt they were a better deal. We both pulled out our credit cards and purchased the binoculars, along with a couple shirts and a hat that said Phinda Forest Lodge. (The hat would be the subject of another unbelievable story that unfolded on our second trip to Africa.) We signed the receipts without paying much attention and hustled outside for our next game drive. One thing I did notice was that in the course of ten minutes, the shopkeeper's disposition became nothing short of giddy. I wondered what the big deal was—we had only spent about $750. I guessed she was delighted that she made such a big sale so quickly.

When we got into the range vehicle, James looked back at us and saw both of us with our new binoculars hanging around our necks. "Wow, you got the good ones," he said. "Can I look through them?" Sure, I said, and passed them forward. James took his first gander through our new binoculars and told us how amazing they were. I thought James' binoculars were nice, but he said someday he wanted to have a pair like ours. In my mind I was thinking that Cindy, Gordon, Leanne, and I were kind of big tippers, so by the time we were done with our safari we would probably tip him enough that he could buy his own. For those next two weeks, we enjoyed Africa much more because we never struggled to see anything. We could see every whisker on a lion's nose, every wrinkle of an elephant's hide, and every fly buzzing around the hyenas as they tore into their kills across the savanna.

All of us wished we could have stayed in Africa longer, but after a few magical weeks, it was time to go home. We went to the airport in Cape Town to begin the long journey home. Before we left, we requested our refund for the VAT tax on all the purchases and gifts we bought while we were in South Africa. Leanne went up to the counter with all of our receipts to process the paperwork and the clerk gave her a receipt back with the amount that would be credited to our credit card, calculated in US dollars. Leanne came over and told me we were getting $500 back. It seemed a little high, but I didn't think much about it at the time.

A week later, Leanne got a phone call from Cindy. She asked if Leanne had seen her credit card bill for the binoculars yet. Leanne told her no, not yet. Cindy dropped the bombshell that the binoculars were not $300—they were $3,000! Leanne wanted to call the gift store in Africa to check the price, but Cindy told her she had already gone online and searched for Swarovski binoculars. She found them on Amazon for over $3,000. *(Go to the link at the end of this chapter to check out the Swarovski binoculars!)*

First the cheetah, then the hyena, while the vultures wait their turn.

Leanne and I both stood there in shock when we did our own online search and saw the price. Now I knew why the woman in the shop was so giddy—she had just made the biggest sale of her life! She probably sold more that one day than the store usually sold in a month (or several). Cindy and Leanne laughed as they remembered how the lodge staff hugged us and said how they would miss all of us. We wondered what all the loving was about, but chalked it up to friendly staff.

After everything settled in and we realized the magnitude

of our mistake, Leanne and I both agreed that it was a painful mistake, but at least we could afford it. Besides, we wanted to only remember all the wonderful things about Africa, and without a doubt, our safari experience was greatly enhanced by having the exceptional binoculars. Instead of letting the mistake taint our experience, we turned it into a positive. We tell the story to all our friends and laugh about how we made such a big mistake. Another good thing about it is that I learned a very, very valuable lesson. When someone says they're going to do something for me, whether at home or traveling, I make sure I understand in detail exactly what the price is and what's included. The result is I don't have many unwanted surprises.

  Clarity is king when you travel, just like cash is king. Take an extra fifteen to thirty seconds and ask a few more questions, no matter where you are. Make sure there is absolute clarity before you give the cab driver the directions to where you want to go. Confirm that he is willing to sit and wait so that you have a cab when you come back out. Get the driver's phone number, program it into your phone, and call it right there to make sure it rings on his phone. When hotel staff gives you a Wi-Fi password, write it down in front of them, and make sure it works so you're not running up and down the elevator trying to get the Wi-Fi working. If someone tells you a meeting time and a location, double and triple check it so there is no ambiguity. The list goes on and on. So much of travel can be enhanced by simply taking a few seconds longer and making sure you have the facts and total clarity.

  Above all, make sure you know the real price when you're looking at Swarovski binoculars! *(Go to the link at the end of this chapter to check out Paul's Africa journey!)*

> **The One Thing:**
> **100% clarity is golden and it will save you a lot of gold!**

paulakers.net/lt-10

Chapter 11

Details

When I did the outline for this book, I came up with over 48 different chapters. There was no way that Paul Akers was going to write a book that long. I'm all about short and simple, cut to the chase, get to the point, and get it over with. As I finished the last few chapters, I noticed there were still a few things that I really needed to discuss, so I decided to add a chapter that summarized some important points and call it "Details."

Everything you're about to read is the result of me observing processes and then asking myself the following two questions:

> **Where is the waste?**
> **How can I improve this process?**

By continually answering these questions, my travel experience is enhanced and more enjoyable. If you develop this same habit and ask these same questions about everything you do, you will experience the benefits of Lean thinking at the highest level. In this chapter I'm simply going to create a heading for every subject and give you a paragraph or two of my thoughts. So let's get going.

1. The perfect workout.

Whenever I travel, it's important that I maintain a routine that makes me feel healthy, vibrant, and alive. Most of us have gone on vacation and gained five to ten pounds, then regretted our laziness and lack of discipline. There is absolutely no reason for that, and I've completely solved that problem by creating a perfect workout I can do anywhere in the world. The first thing I do when I get up in the morning is drop to my knees and do 100 push-ups and 200 sit-ups. That's basically it. This eight-minute daily routine (that I never miss) keeps me tuned up and ready to go. Other than that, I make it a point to move at least 10,000 steps per day. That's

On the beach of Phuket doing 100 push-ups everyday. No excuses!

all I do to stay in top physical shape. *(Go to the link at the end of this chapter to learn Paul's travel workouts!)*

2. How to eat healthy.

Eat plants, not foods made in plants. Don't open a package, eat only fresh produce and fish and you will thrive on vacation. Everywhere I go, I seek out all the beautiful vegetables and fruit that are readily available around the world. The key is you have to train your eyes to see these great healthy foods. Once you've done that you will find them with great ease. Just today, I checked into my hotel in Astana, Kazakhstan, and they gave me a beautiful fruit basket with at least fifteen different pieces of fruit. Why was I so fortunate to have this? Because I have made it very clear to everyone I know that this is what I eat and I do not want sugary or packaged foods.

Checking into my hotel, they know I am a fruit maniac and they had this delicious bowl of fruit waiting for me in my hotel room. One of the keys to life is to be remarkable, so people cannot forget you.

You couldn't spend more than an hour with me before discovering the clarity I have regarding how I fuel my body. My friends and colleagues definitely know this. En route to Kazakhstan, I stopped in Frankfurt, Germany, for a few hours. My good friend Michael Althoff and his girlfriend came to see me at the airport. I was shocked when Michael handed me an ice-cold smoothie out of a cooler he brought with him. He knew my health was so important to me that he made and carried three smoothies with him for more than an hour on a high-speed train just so I could eat healthy food when my feet touched the ground in Germany. *(Go to the link at the end of this chapter to see Michael providing Paul his smoothie.)*

Michael Althoff my good friend from Germany traveled two hours to deliver two fresh smoothies for me in Frankfurt, Germany

On another recent trip, to Easter Island, our bus stopped

for a few minutes so we could grab some snacks at a little store on the side of the road. Not me! I looked for other options. I saw a lady selling fresh produce on the side of the road and went over and bought a bag of fresh tomatoes and some tangerines. While everyone else was fueling themselves with packaged crap from the mainland, I was nurturing my body with beautiful fruit grown in the island's rich soil.

First thing I did when I got off the plane on Easter Island is look for fresh fruit, vegetables, and made some new friends.

Throughout this book I have tried to explain my thought processes and how Lean thinking has influenced the way I travel. The top priority in the Lean world is improving quality. We are always asking how we can deliver more value to the customer by improving quality and simultaneously driving down costs. Understanding the value of quality is what allows me to so easily make healthy decisions while others are so easily tempted by what is cheap and fast. Eating correctly is not an incidental activity or afterthought—it is my top priority. In this case, my customer is my body and the only thing I will offer to that customer is high-quality, healthy food. *(Go to the link at the end of this chapter to learn more about eating healthy while traveling.)*

3. My health is everything.

If you adopt this mindset you will be shocked by how easy it is to take care of your health when you're traveling. If you don't have your health, travel can be difficult and you surely won't enjoy it as much as you would if you

Strong body, Strong minds

were in great physical health. (If you're a person who is full of excuses and you want to tell me how difficult it is, I guarantee it will be difficult.) I never have a difficult time. No matter where I am traveling, maintaining perfect health is easy and an absolute pleasure. Simple routines like always carrying several apples and some nuts in my backpack make sure I'm always prepared in the rare event I can't find something healthy.

You've heard me talk about my love for Kazakhstan and how much I appreciate and love the culture and the amazing hospitality of this great country. When I was there on my birthday in May, they had a great dinner to celebrate Arman's, Metin's and my birthdays. I stood up and made a toast. I told them I felt like I had Kazakh blood, that I really felt I was part of the Kazakh people and it was like home for me. Aydin said I was not just Kazakh, but I was also Naiman! He said that the Naiman people are a tribe in Kazakhstan that lives by the water and eats fish. So, I am a Naiman—I focus on my health and only put the best nutrients in it. If you think like a Naiman your body will love you for it.

4. How to load a bus, train, boat, or plane.

I wrote about this in Chapter 6, but I want to give a little more detail here. It may seem like a strange subject, but believe me, there are some very important nuances to understand when you're getting on these four different modes of transportation. For example, if you're loading the bus that takes you from the airplane to the terminal, you want to be the last one on. Most people rush to get off the plane and onto the bus, then they just sit there while everybody else gets on. Slow down! The last people off the plane will be the last people to get on the bus, which puts them closest to the door. They will be the first ones to get off and reach the passport clearance zone. Customs can take a long time, so it's best to be at the front of the line there. Waiting a

Position is everything!!!

Be observant when picking your seats. You don't want to miss anything!

little longer on the plane makes that happen more easily.

The same thing applies to the rental car bus. If you ever want to waste twenty to thirty minutes, make sure you're the last one off the bus at the rental car office. Rental car lines are ridiculously long and they move really slowly. Take a spot by the door of the bus so you can be the first one in line to get the keys and the first one to drive away.

There are a few exceptions to this rule, however. When you're on a bus tour that is going to last more than half an hour and you want to have a great view, you should be the first one on the bus so you can sit at the front and have the best vantage point. (You might need to show up twenty minutes before the bus leaves to get the seat.) If you're planning to board a train in Japan, you want to sit as close to the bus's luggage area as possible, so that when it is time to get off, you can quickly grab your bags and get to the platform. Japanese trains operate with high precision and they wait for no one. If you're a busy executive and you know you need to make a lot of phone calls during a long bus ride, it might be best to sit in the very back where you won't be disturbing everyone with your phone calls and communications.

You can choose which side of a bus or plane to sit on based on where the best views are going to be. When we flew from Santiago, Chile, down to Patagonia, I made sure I sat on the left side of the plane so I could view the mountains more clearly. When we were traveling to see the glaciers in Patagonia, I sat on the left side of the bus because I knew the glaciers would be on the left side of the road we were taking. It only took a few clicks in Google Maps to find this out. People on the right side of the bus were struggling to take pictures, but not me. The important thing is to think about everything. If you are in a particularly hot (or cold) climate and the sun is going to be shining on one side or the other, consider that too. Air-conditioners on buses do not always work well, nor do the heaters. Pick the correct side so you don't bake or freeze.

I also very carefully observe patterns of people getting on and off tour buses. I even ask guides and drivers where to sit because that local first-hand knowledge can be invaluable. Little details like these can make all the difference in the world.

On a boat, the best place to be is in the center because there's less motion. You should also consider how cold it's going to be. Tourists tend to rush to the open area on top of the boat so they have a better view, but it is often very cold on the water. When they get cold and go downstairs to look for a seat, all of them are taken. With nowhere to sit, they have to go freeze their butts off on the deck for the hour they're on the boat.

You already know my thoughts about loading a plane: always be the last one on, so you have the best opportunity to get the best seat. Don't rush to get on—you don't want to sit on those tiny little seats for any longer than you have to! The waiting area is much more comfortable than the plane.

Thinking about these tales can really make a big difference. You can be lackadaisical about all the details—perhaps it's not a big deal to you—but they have made my travel so much more enjoyable because all the little things add up to make big improvements. *(Go to the link at the end of this chapter to learn Paul's top travel tips.)*

5. How to book a flight.

There are two good ways to book flights. One is to use a website like Expedia that stores all your information (credit card, passport number, etc.) and only takes a few seconds to book a flight anywhere in the world. The site is easy to navigate, prices are generally reasonable, and it retains records and receipts of upcoming and past trips. The only disadvantage is that when you go to upgrade on the day of your flight, the airlines will not always allow you to do this because the flight was booked through a third party. *(Go to the link at the end of this chapter to learn more about the Expedia App.)*

That brings us to the second way to book flights: to book them directly with the airlines themselves. If you book directly, you have more flexibility in terms of last-minute upgrades. This can be very important, but if the website of the carrier that you're working with is not easy to navigate or cumbersome you could easily spend twenty minutes booking a flight that you could book on Expedia in fifteen seconds. For long international flights especially, you have to weigh your options and determine the value of your time the length of the flight and the options that you think you might need. I have a few airlines that I book directly with even though their websites suck, because they will not allow me to upgrade to business class if I book somewhere else. This happens the most with long international flights. At the end of the day, though, Expedia is my go-to site because it is fast, easy, economical, has all my information, and is more effective than any travel agent I've used in the past or ever will use in the future. It is stellar in all regards.

6. How to book a hotel.

I talked about this in Chapter 5. The last minute is when the best deals are almost always available.

7. The travel map.

I really recommend having a map that allows you to see where you've been and where you'd like to go. About five years ago, I ordered a large world map (about 3' x 4') online and mounted it on one-inch thick foam board I bought at Lowe's. The insulated foam board is sold in

My travel map is one of my favorite things. It gives me an opportunity to reflect on all the wonderful places I have been and all the wonderful places I still need to see.

4' x 8' sheets, so I cut it with a standard utility knife and used FastCap's SpeedTape to stick the map to the foam board. I built a custom vertical-grain frame for it and hung it up, then I started putting push pins and all the countries I've been to around the world. The standard red, green, and yellow pushpins that you buy at the office supply store were a little small, so I took red Fastcaps (also from my company) and put them on top of the pushpins, which highlighted and accentuated the map points and countries. *(Go to the link at the end of this chapter to see Paul's travel map & more information about SpeedTape and FastCaps.)*

8. All the scams.
As far as I'm concerned, the mileage programs for most airlines are total scams and a waste of time. While I still put my mileage numbers in when I book flights, I can't remember the last time I was really able to use my miles. There always seems to be some exception or the airline wants to send me on a crazy route, like going through Phoenix on my way to Alaska (departing at Bellingham). The next biggest scam is when you go to a car rental company and they want you to buy extra insurance or prepay for the fuel. You've got to be kidding me! First of all, your insurance policy for your normal car generally has some kind of rental car coverage and the credit card you rent the car with often does too. Prepaying for fuel is a bad idea because the companies charge you extra high prices if you return the car without a full tank. The only way it possibly makes sense is if you return the car without a drop of fuel left in the tank, and nobody does that. The rental car companies know this and make huge amounts of money off of people's ignorance.

9. The perfect room check-out: never lose a thing.
I can't tell you the number of times I used to check out of one hotel and into a different one, only to realize I left my charger, my toothbrush, or my razor behind. Now, this rarely, if ever happens to me. I don't forget anything because

I always put my suitcase in the hotel doorway and then go back through the room with my hands empty and carefully scan everything.

I have a simple process that almost 100 percent guarantees I never leave a thing in the room. First, I pack up my bag and my backpack, roll them out to the door, and use them to hold the door open. Then with both my hands free, I walk through the entire room and bathroom one more time, looking under the bed and carefully checking to see if I left anything plugged in, or in the closet, safe, or desk. I'm not holding my suitcase, my coat, or anything else, which allows me to focus on seeing things I've left behind. I start in one corner of the room and systematically work my way out to the door. This has been invaluable for me.

10. How to check into your room.

Hotels are notoriously slow for checking you in, and why it takes them five to ten minutes to give you your room key is a mystery to me. I can check in for my flight in about thirty seconds at an electronic kiosk, but hotels go through this laboriously long process to get you the keys and get you checked in.

Whenever you unpack in the hotel room do not spread out. Keep everything in one area. This requires less time to set up and to pack up when it's time to go.

One technique I use to speed up the process is to walk up to the counter with my credit card and license in hand and tell the clerks I'm in a little bit of a hurry can we get this done really quickly. This puts a little pressure on them so they're not dillydallying like they normally do. Next, when I get into my room, I'm very thoughtful about the way I unpack. I don't scatter my stuff all over the room. The more you scatter, the longer it's going to take you to pack it up, so be thoughtful and carefully unpack. Doing this will save you so much time and hassle. *(Go to the link at the end of this chapter to learn how to pack Lean and Lean key tracking.)*

11. Your phone and the rental car.

Driving an unfamiliar car in an unfamiliar city can be sheer chaos if you don't prepare. I have learned it pays to slow down, get all the stuff worked out, and then I can drive confidently to my next location. Long before I get into my rental car—while the plane is taxiing up to the terminal, in fact—I program where I'm going into my phone. I never drive out of the rental car lot until my phone has determined my location and knows exactly where to guide me.

Set up correctly before you leave so you can enjoy your drive. When I get into the car, I put my seat belt on, review the controls on the dash and steering wheel, and check the map on my phone to get a basic layout of my surroundings. Then I can just enjoy driving and not worrying about finding the cruise control or the air conditioning. Make sure your phone has a good place to rest on the dashboard or console and plug it into your phone charger so its battery doesn't drain down as you drive. I always make sure my backpack is in the driver's seat so if I need to get anything out, it is within easy reach. Also, pay very close attention to where the gas stations are when departing the airport because you will need to fill the car up when you return. You don't want to get ripped off by the rental companies. I always rent the smallest, cheapest car possible. Small cars are much easier to park and get around in, plus they use less fuel. When you do refuel, pay attention to the gas gauge—it has a small arrow to indicate what side the fuel tank is on. This will save you a little bit of hassle when refueling.

If there isn't someone in the lot when you return your car, take a picture of the mileage with your phone so when you walk up to the counter inside the airport you have

Make sure everything is ready before you drive out of the parking lot

Waze is the ultimate navigation program for Driving

Take a picture of the mileage on your rental car

the information easily accessible. The same process applies to dropping off a car as for checking out of a hotel room. Get all your stuff out of the car and when your hands are free, go back through the entire car, checking carefully between and underneath the seats. The key is to have your hands free so you can concentrate and focus. *(Go to the link at the end of this chapter to learn how to Lean out your rental car!)*

12. Music in the bathroom.

Music, music, music! It can set the mood for my entire life. I work out to it, I shower to it, and I fall sleep to it.

I have to thank my good friend Michael Althoff for this one. When I stayed at his home he often let me have his master bedroom. In the morning, I would wake up, turn on the bathroom light, and beautiful music would come out of the stereo system he had built into his bathroom. The second the bathroom light switched on, rock 'n' roll would fill the room energizing me as I showered and shaved. I thought it was so cool because you didn't even have to think about anything—it was all automatic. The music set the tone for the entire morning. As a result of Michael's example, I always travel with the Bose SoundLink Mini speaker system, which I play when I'm in the bathroom in the morning. It's a little heavy and bulky to carry with me around the world, but it is worth it. I love having high-quality music when I'm traveling—it makes me feel like I'm at home.

13. How to be an educated traveler.

This subject is not just about being an educated traveler—it's about being educated, period. The key to understanding the feel of a place you're visiting is to go to YouTube and watch five or six videos about it. I do this all the time and it helps me grasp the culture, the people, and what is important to see in a matter of minutes. My main example comes from when I went to Easter Island. I wanted to

YouTube App

understand what the island was all about and I could have easily read about it, but I watched a documentary and it gave me such insight into what I was going to see and experience. Because I knew what to expect and look for, the whole trip was that much richer. YouTube is great when it comes to educating yourself on just about every subject you could imagine. If I want to know how to run correctly, swim correctly, learn a new computer process, or find out about an exotic place I'm traveling to, I go to YouTube. *(Go to the link at the end of this chapter and learn how to utilize YouTube!)*

What better person to ask question about the city than a taxi driver?

14. The knowledgeable taxi cab driver.

There is no one who knows more about a city than a taxicab driver. When you get in a cab, don't just sit there like a bump on a log—ask the cab driver where the best place to go is, where the best restaurants are, where the cool spots that you can't miss are. Even more importantly, you should ask the drivers where they're from. This usually turns into a very interesting cultural exchange as they tell you about their life in Nigeria, India, Afghanistan, or all the other interesting places people come from to find a better life. I learned this concept from the book *How to Win Friends and Influence People*. The most important thing you'll ever do for any human beings is to let them tell you about themselves and learn their names. It not about you, it's about them.

15. One, two, three, this is not a rehearsal.

I live my life by a few powerful concepts. One of them is: life is not a rehearsal. So many people think that they'll do something tomorrow, next week, or in a couple years. The time is now! Every second is precious. Make the most of every second in

Embrace life. Embrace the people that you meet.

your life and stop making excuses on why you can't do things. Start saying yes. Your life will be remarkable.

When I meet people and they invite me to come to their country and visit them in their home, I don't think to myself, well, maybe. I take action. I look at my calendar and say I'll be there in three weeks. The next thing you know, I'm in Portugal and Assel is showing me around beautiful Lisbon and all the wonderful castles of Sentra. This has happened to me over and over again in my life; that's why I have friends all over the world. I'm always figuring out how to say yes. Life is very short. The sooner you figure this out, the better off you'll be.

When Michael and his girlfriend met me in Germany they immediately took me to a fruit stand with fresh fruit and vegetables. We expect high expectations for yourself, people will embrace them and help you met them.

16. Embrace the world.

When I first went to Japan, I remember Brad telling me, "Don't be judgmental. Don't go into these factories and find all the problems. Be open—learn and experience all you can, because if you go in with the critical attitude you'll miss the best stuff." If you're always looking to pick things apart and find the problems, you're going to miss the beauty that the world has to offer.

Learn, learn, learn. Experience, experience, experience. There is so much to fill your life with that is positive.

Always look for the positive. People comment to me over and over again: "Paul you're so positive," "You're so nice to everyone," or "You go out of your way to learn people's names and recognize the waiters, the bus boys, the bellmen, and the people who would seemingly be insignificant." That is correct! I love people. I love to acknowledge them and I love encouraging them. This is the way I approach everything in life, especially when I'm in someone else's country. My favorite thing to do when I'm in Kazakhstan is visit the canteens where all the workers eat. The women who prepare the food are so hard-working and so diligent, and they do a great job. I always go back in the kitchen and thank them for the wonderful food and get some really cool pictures with all of them. They are always a little shocked that there's this American celebrity in their country who is taking the time to acknowledge the workers in the kitchen. *(Go to the link at the end of this chapter to see Paul's journey through India!)*

17. Patience and the leopard.

In Africa they call this "Pants in a tree" If you're patient the leopard will put on quite a show for you.

Everyone knows the old saying that "patience is a virtue." It may be true, but I guarantee you, patience is not in my DNA, nor am I particularly proficient at it. I have, however, learned to improve in this area. I try to do the opposite of what most people do and exercise patience. Being patient has produced some of my most fabulous memories. My favorite examples of this all occurred in Africa when we were on safari. For each of them, our time spent waiting for something dramatic to happen paid off. Each time, while we sat in our range vehicle with no action occurring, three or four other range vehicles drove away impatient and frustrated, but I insisted we wait.

As a result, we saw several spectacular sights occur right in front of us. The first one was a leopard that had made a kill and carried it up a tree for safekeeping. As we watched, the leopard climbed back up the tree and

Because we were patient and waiting over an hour, we saw the cheetah make the kill, the hyena chase the cheetah away, and the vultures patiently wait for the hyenas to be finish so they could get their turn.

dragged the carcass down on the ground right in front of our range vehicle, so close I could've reached out and touch the leopard. (Yes, it's all on video!)

Mother and her cubs reunited and en route to dinner, while we followed in the truck

The second one was watching a cheetah that had also just made a kill. After about an hour had gone by, a pack of hyenas ran towards it and the cheetah ran off and left the kill. We got to see the hyenas tear into it right in front of us. Simultaneously, we saw vultures jockeying intensely to get the meat while the hyenas chased them away over and over again. It was unbelievable and we were the only ones to see it.

The third one was a female lion that had lost her cubs after she made a kill. She was yelling loudly, hoping they would hear her and return to her. Unfortunately, she had left them several miles away up on a little knoll and they could not hear her. After an hour of her yelping she left the kill and searched for her cubs. We followed her along the road for a half hour and we saw them reunited. It was amazing. The lioness then led them back to the kill with the rest of the pride and they and ate for another hour. Once again, everyone else missed the drama.

The greatest one of all happened when we went to the Maasai Mara National Reserve to see the wildebeest and zebra migration. Thousands of the animals cross the Mara river at one time, all while trying to avoid the crocodiles waiting intently for them. You

Notice the stripes in the center of the crocodiles...That was a zebra. We saw 24 zebra taken in an hour. Our guide said he had never seen anything like it, in 20 years.

never know for sure when this crossing is going to happen, but our ranger had a sense that it would that day so we parked on the riverbank and waited. . . . and waited. . . . and waited. Other range vehicles came and went but none stayed with us. After about two hours the crossing began right in front of us and we had a front-row seat. It was a world-class sighting.

All of these events are recorded in my Africa video and they are sheer drama. I was able to capture these memories because I did the opposite of what other people do and I exercised extreme patience. Now I have memories that will last me a lifetime.

18. Time zone magic.
This is such a small thing, but it makes a big difference. The second you get on the plane when you're going to a new time zone, immediately change the time on your phone and your watch. The sooner you start thinking about the new time zone you'll be living in, the sooner your brain will adjust, making jet lag a non-issue. For instance, if you're going to Germany and as the plane takes off you realize that they would be going to bed in about six hours, you should start thinking about sleeping in six hours. I would take a sleeping pill to start switching my clock before we even land in Germany. Then when I get there, I've already rested and I've begun to assimilate into the new time zone. This can make a huge difference if you do it right. The first night I take another sleeping pill to make sure I sleep through the night so the next day my body has clearly adjusted to the new time zone.

I do the same thing in reverse when I come home. I make sure to sleep when I'm supposed to be sleeping on the plane and take sleeping pills the first two nights after I return home. I don't want to be awake in the middle of the night. I learned this trick from a friend of mine based in Argentina who travels extensively around the world. Teddy taught it to me fifteen years ago and it literally changed my life in regard to jet lag. I don't even know what the word means anymore.

19. Smile and sell some flowers.

I have talked repeatedly about the importance of greeting people with a smile and being friendly. Here's a small backstory that will give you some insight as to where I'm coming from: When I was thirteen or fourteen years old, I used to sell flowers on the corner in National City (near San Diego). After school every day I'd be dropped off on a corner with a bucket of flowers to sell. Every hour, the driver would have to come back and replenish my flowers because I had sold them all. I was the top salesperson five times over. No one could even come close to selling the amount of flowers I did.

I learned the power of smiling when I was just 13 years old selling flowers on a street corner. Not only did it enhance the quality of my life but it enhanced my bank account dramatically.

I was earning $40-$70 a night back in 1973 and would come home every night and iron my money to make it all flat. I made so much money that when I was fifteen, I bought my first car and sailboat. My driver was astounded and couldn't figure out how I did it. It was so simple—all I did was smile and ask everybody nicely who stopped at the stop sign after leaving the freeway, "Hello, would you like to buy some flowers?" With a grin from ear to ear. I guess everybody thought I looked innocent and cute. They would quickly hand me a five-dollar bill and I would hand them a bunch of roses as they drove off. Smile, smile, smile. Be nice—you will have a much better life.

Do people tell you that you're a positive source?

20. Never miss a sunset.

Forget about all the material things in life. All the things that we think are important—nice cars, nice homes, expensive vacations—all pale in comparison to quietly sitting on the beach as the sun goes down. When I see the sunset or the sunrise anywhere in the world, I pause and I have a grateful heart. How lucky I am to experience this wonder every day of my life! *(Go to the link at the end of this chapter to see beautiful drone images from Paul's travels around the world.)*

My soul is calmed when I sit and watch the close of everyday, while I experience nature's finality.

The One Thing:
Look for patterns.

paulakers.net/lt-11

Chapter 12

It's a Very Small World

As a public speaker, I always start off my talks by saying, "I have a true confession, I don't like Lean." Then I pause, giving the audience enough time to wonder why they hired me to come talk to them about Lean and tell them what a big difference it can make in their organization. Finally, I tell them the truth: "I love Lean!"

I really do love Lean. It has given me so much in life. My passion for continuous improvement has connected me with people all over the world. People see me in action and they see my effectiveness and all-around efficiency and are drawn to the concept of continuous improvement. They reach out to me and the next thing you know, we develop friendships that improve and enrich their lives and mine.

People gravitate toward those who are passionate and positive. When you approach life with deep passion and you look for the best in others, it is inevitable that your life will be filled with adventure and happiness. You will make new friends wherever you travel. You will never forget them and they will never forget you.

Up to this point, I've told you travel stories with epic drama, colossal misunderstandings, and costly mistakes. All of these allowed me to learn and improve so that my travel experiences would grow the smile on my face with each passing trip. Now I'm going to tell you a story that makes the world seem so tiny it will be hard to believe.

As I said in the last chapter, our first trip to Africa was amazing. There is a saying that once you get the dirt of Africa between your toes, you will never get it out and you will have to return. We got the dirt not only in our toes, but also in our shoes, clothes, and everywhere else! So one year later, we headed back again, this time to explore Tanzania and Kenya. Our second trip was easier because we had some idea of what to expect. We were much more comfortable with Africa's simplicity and wildness. On the first trip, we had come to love the people of this continent. We made new friends and stayed in touch with them continually. We kept in contact with the rangers and lots of the people we met. It became normal for me to talk to someone in Africa on a weekly basis. Africa was no longer a distant and mysterious land; it was now a part of me. *(Go to the link at the end of this chapter to see Paul and Leanne's trip to Kenya!)*

Landing at Lake Manyara.

The first few days in Tanzania, we visited Lake Manyara National Park. To get there, we flew into a small dirt runway where our ranger, Peter, picked us up in an open Land Cruiser. We spent the better part of the first day wandering through the beautiful park over remote dirt roads. We made it to &Beyond's Lake Manyara Tree Lodge, just as the sun was going down. We chose &Beyond again because our first experience was so exceptional. *(Go to the link at the end of this chapter learn more about &Beyond!)*

The resort was called a tree lodge because the rooms were built up in the trees on stilts. They had no glass windows, only simple screening to keep the animals out. This was somewhat unsettling because the area is famous for its tree-climbing lions. The first night, however, it was not lions that concerned us, it was leopards. Most of the night we could hear a leopard panting outside our window, and the only thing between him and us was a thin piece of screen and the sheet covering our trembling bodies. Experiences like this are why I love Africa. They can make you a little tense, but you become addicted to the adventure.

The old land rover coming down the road, caught my attention because Toyota is everywhere in Africa. Little did I know in the middle of nowhere there would be friends from a distant land.

The next morning, we got up

early so that we could take a sunrise game drive and have breakfast overlooking the hot springs and beautiful Lake Manyara. At five o'clock, the porter came and knocked on our screen door with hot coffee and biscuits. We had just enough time to take a steamy outdoor shower (with no protection from the wild animals—just me and my bare ass and that panting leopard!) before heading out for the drive.

You can live every moment, every word of the following story. It is all documented in high definition. I produced a series of videos for each day we were in Africa, so the story can unfold in front of you in living color. Each video is professionally produced and will transport you to our Land Cruiser on the dirt roads of Africa. Each day, I took the video, did the narration and all the editing just-in-time, using one-piece flow so there was never any batch work. I produced the videos while the stories were fresh in my mind. If I didn't like the camera angle or the narration or the lighting, the very next day I could improve my process and thus improve the quality of the videos—day after day continuous improvement. Most people would ask how it's possible to do so much. It's easy, because Lean thinking makes everything I do easy and fun, and the result is I get much more done than most people could ever dream of. *(Go to the link at the end of this chapter to watch Paul and Leanne on a safari!)*

My wife and I were getting ready to go when a Maasai warrior showed up at our front door holding his spear. He walked us down a sandy trail, scanning the bushes around us for lions and leopards. After the hundred-yard "walk of terror," we met Peter and climbed into the open Land Cruiser. It was a chilly morning, but he had a heavy blanket to put over us as we enjoyed the early morning sights and sounds. The only thing we had to worry about was lions jumping into the open truck and eating us as we meandered through the jungle.

Having breakfast in Lake Manyara. Not a soul anywhere except for hippos and flamingos.

For the next hour we observed the wildlife as the forest came to life. Eventually, we stopped on a small ridge where Peter set up a small folding table and three chairs so we could eat breakfast and watch the sun come up over the lake.

We sat down to eat a delicious meal of crepes, eggs, fresh fruit, hot coffee, and hot chocolate. I thought to myself how crazy it was to be 10,000 miles from home, in the middle of nowhere, enjoying wonderful food, solitude, and nature in such a beautiful setting—it couldn't get any better than that!

Up to this point, there had been absolutely no one else around. We weren't in a place where there were cars passing by every three to five minutes. You could go for hours without seeing anyone. It was just the land, the animals, and us. Or so we thought.

After a few minutes, I heard the sound of another range vehicle approaching from over the ridge. As it came closer, I realized it was not the typical Toyota Land Cruiser that is so common in Africa. It was an older Range Rover from England, something you rarely see anymore because they're just not very reliable. (Toyota, thanks to the company's Lean and continuous improvement efforts, is famous for its quality and reliability. Its Land Cruiser has become the vehicle of choice for traveling in rural parts of Africa. No other brand can survive the harsh African terrain.)

This Range Rover had a certain charm to it, and it kind of felt like I was watching the movie *Out of Africa* as it approached. Being the videographer and storyteller that I am, I pulled out my camera to record the moment. Capturing a ten-second clip of this vehicle as it crossed in front of me would help convey the romance of traveling across Africa. However, as the truck approached, it slowed down and stopped right next to me. I kept the camera rolling as the man driving the car stopped and said good morning. I greeted him and told him what a cool truck he had. I said I was filming a little bit of it because it looked so interesting. The man was very friendly and did not mind at all.

What came next surprised me. He asked if I had been to

Phinda Forest Lodge. We were at least a thousand miles from the lodge, and I had forgotten I was wearing the Phinda Forest Lodge hat I bought the year before in South Africa (the same place we bought our famous "$350" Swarovski binoculars). I told him we had gone there last year. I wondered how he knew where Phinda Forest Lodge was, since it was in a place just as remote as where we were in Tanzania.

Then, to my total shock, the man told us his son works there as a ranger. I asked if his name was James, and he and his wife both exclaimed, "Yes!" We told him how James was our first ranger when we came to Africa. Then they asked, "Are you Paul and Leanne?" We were stunned and answered yes! "We thought we recognized you from the videos you made and the iPole you gave him," he explained.

James' father pulled out his cell phone and dialed his son, who was in another remote African country on holiday. When James answered, his father said, "You will never believe who we just met in the middle of nowhere in Tanzania—Paul and Leanne Akers!" James' father handed me the phone and James and I went crazy with laughter and surprise. All of us couldn't believe what had just happened. What were the chances we would be in Africa again and meet his parents at this remote location so early in the morning? It is such a small world.

Meeting Jame's parents was a shock to say the least.

A week later we were in Kenya, far out in the middle of nowhere, staying at Klein's Camp, another of &Beyond's resorts. We were in route to the Maasai Mara game reserve because we wanted to see the great wildebeest migration. In person, the migration was stunning. We could see at least 100,000 wildebeests, stretching out as far as we could see. I asked Seleu, our ranger, if we could leave the road and drive right into the center of them and let the herd envelope us. He said, "Sure, why not?" I kept my camera rolling as I hung outside the jeep to capture the drama of chasing wildebeests at forty miles an hour. I was so caught up in everything that was going on that I didn't even realize when my hat blew off my head. The hat that had brought me together with James' parents was now lying somewhere in the middle of the Maasai Mara. I was disappointed, but I knew there must be a reason! Life is not just happenstance. There is so much to explore and learn. We are all so connected and life is doing everything in its power to bring us all together.

The subtitle of this book is *Travel Light with a Full Heart*. As I bring this book to a close I must tell you, my heart is full. Travel has been one of the most important elements of my own self-development. I first became attracted to travel because of my father Harry Akers and his intense pursuit of adventure. From an early age, he would load my mother, brother, and me up in our Studebaker station wagon and drive across the country visiting every state and national park across America. My best memories are sitting in the front seat on my mom's lap, chewing on the dashboard as we rambled down the road. (I managed to put a consistent row of teeth marks all the way across the front console and would give anything to have a picture of that dashboard—such tasty memories.)

My dad was whispering in my ear since a baby: travel, adventure, explore the world.

Traveling with my mom and dad in Alaska

It seemed like every summer we went on some wild adventure somewhere in the US, Canada or Mexico. One summer, my dad loaded six Boy Scouts plus me into Don Longbottom's old Dodge van and we drove over 3,000 miles to Canada for the Boy Scout National Jamboree. For a group of 13 year old boys, this was high adventure. Along the way, we even picked up two young hippie girls who were hitchhiking across America and gave them a ride for over 800 miles. We talked about everything with them—from sex, drugs, and rock 'n roll, to becoming vegetarian. These girls made such a big impression on me. They were living life.

Our old family Studebaker. We traveled all over the United States visiting national parks. My dad did a fantastic job of instilling in me a sense of adventure and the desire to travel and make as many friends as possible... I just wish I had a picture of all my teeth marks across the front dash board.

They were out on some great adventure and they weren't letting any inhibitions hold them back. I think my dad thought maybe the kids could learn something from this, and learn we did! They even convinced me to become a vegetarian and stop eating sugar for about one year. (My dad also got a kick out of the fact that we were a gaggle of horny thirteen-year-old boys with two cute twenty year-old girls in the car and we didn't know what to do with ourselves.) Between my dad and those young girls, I came away with a burning sense of adventure that all the water in Lake Michigan could not extinguish. Wow, what a ride.

I made it as an Eagle Scout when I was only 14 years old...Which prepared me perfectly to travel the world.

My taste for adventure travel runs deep in my family history. My grandfather left Greece in 1913 and immigrated to the United States to find a better life for his family. My dad was highly involved in the Boy Scouts with me and I became an Eagle Scout. Talk about burning resourcefulness and self-reliance into my psyche at an early age! I was continually active and spent much of my free time hiking up some massive mountain like Mt. Whitney, canoeing down the Colorado River, descending into the Grand Canyon, or trekking up the Zion Narrows.

A well-traveled friend of mine from South Africa once told

me that if you want to remove all bigotry, racism, and political tensions from the world, all you need to do is get people to travel. In the process you will gain a deep appreciation and understanding of different cultures, languages and religions. I couldn't agree more. People are basically good, kindhearted, willing to help, and desiring friendships and understanding almost everywhere in the world.

One of my favorite illustrations of this comes from the Kazakh people. I have spent so much time in Kazakhstan and I've never felt such warm hospitality from any other group of people. My Kazakh friends explained to me that the reason they are such an open and giving people is because their ancestors were nomads living in tents in the middle of very hostile climates. They would go months without seeing anyone, so when someone did wander across their pastures they would welcome them in with open arms and treat them like family. This is how the Kazakh people learned about what was going on in the outside world. This is how they stimulated their minds.

That's what travel does—it stimulates your mind and warms your heart. If sometime in the future you should stumble across my Phinda Forest Hat in the middle of Kenya, please come into my tent, sit down and enjoy a meal. I want to know about your adventures and your travels to distant lands. Tell me what you have learned and I will tell you about my journey and all my wonderful friends. As my dad always said, "Life is an adventure and a life filled with travel is the best adventure in the world!"

I always end my show The American Innovator with these words: "Life is an adventure. Go out and learn and improve. You can make a difference. We can change the world!" People always ask me why I make videos, write books, and make almost everything I do available for free. The answer is really simple: my dad taught me to love life and to share it with everyone. He expected nothing in return, but he relished the twinkle in someone's eyes when they discovered something they didn't know. I'm just doing what my dad modeled for me. Like my father, I get great satisfaction when I see other people learn and improve their lives. So go out and learn and improve. We can change the world!

> **The One Thing:**
> We are connected and traveling to distant lands is the thread that brings us closer together. Whatever you do, travel light with a full heart.

paulakers.net/lt-12

Where it all began, Paul's first book on Lean Manufactoring! Now the winner of *The Shingo Research and Professional Publication Award*

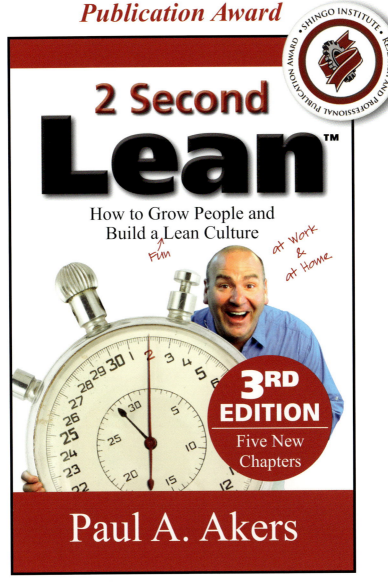

Check out Paul's 2 Second Lean book for FREE online at paulakers.net

Learn how Paul applied Lean principles to his health and started
Aging in Reverse

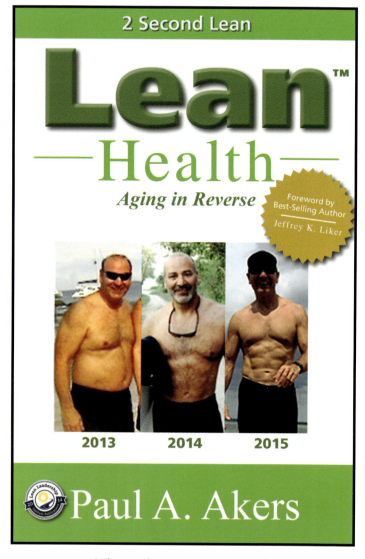

Check out Paul's Lean Health book for FREE online at paulakers.net